Two studies on unemployment
among educated young people

TWO STUDIES ON

unemployment among educated young people

Part I
Unemployment among educated
young people in the developed
market-economy countries
Simone Morio

Part II
Unemployment among educated
young people in the French-speaking
developing countries
Yarrise Zoctizoum

Published in 1980 by the United Nations
Educational, Scientific and Cultural Organization
7 Place de Fontenoy, 75700 Paris
Composed by Solent Typesetting, Otterbourne, United Kingdom
Printed by Imprimerie de la Manutention, Mayenne, France

ISBN 92-3-101618-0
French Edition: 92-3-201618-4
Spanish edition: 92-3-303618-8

Preface

A major aim of Unesco's Youth Programme is to elucidate the problems and aspirations of young people in the contemporary world. To do this, information is collected, analysed and disseminated on issues of major concern to youth. One such issue is the unemployment of young people, an acute problem in many developing and industrialized countries. Numerous publications have been issued and meetings held on this subject; among the latter was the Regional Meeting in Europe on the theme: 'The Effects of the Economic Situation on the Access of Young People to Education, Culture and Work' that Unesco sponsored in Venice from 7 to 11 November 1977.

The present publication concentrates on a specific aspect of the problem: unemployment among educated young people. Furthermore, it limits treatment of this aspect of the problem to countries in two regions of the world, namely Africa and Western Europe. Although the approach was thus thematically focused and geographically limited, it is hoped the problem has been presented both concretely and completely enough for these studies to be of interest to readers concerned about other aspects of youth unemployment and/or working in other parts of the world.

Being well aware that unemployment is a complex economic and social phenomenon which cannot be explained in a simplistic way, the authors have tried to relate the problem of the unemployment of young people to the content, objectives and types of education received.

Part I, which deals with the industrialized countries, was written by Ms S. Morio. Part II, which analyses the situation in Africa, was prepared by Mr Y. Zoctizoum. Both authors are young sociologists who were themselves unemployed during a certain period of their working careers.

The authors are responsible for the choice and presentation of the facts contained in this book and for the opinions expressed therein, which are not necessarily those of Unesco and do not commit the Organization.

Contents

Preface

PART II
UNEMPLOYMENT AMONG EDUCATED YOUNG PEOPLE
IN THE FRENCH-SPEAKING DEVELOPING COUNTRIES

Yarrise Zoctizoum

Unemployment among educated young people in the developed market-economy countries

Simone Morio

Introduction

Unemployment among young people who have received a secondary or university education seems today, in the great majority of developed countries, to pose a very serious problem which is challenging preconceived ideas about the general question of unemployment among young people.

Only a few years ago, this question principally concerned young people who had little or no education, and the classic theory blamed insufficient training (more or less equated with a low level of education) for the difficulties experienced by these young people in finding jobs. Now the increasing numbers of young unemployed in a new category—'graduates'— have revealed the need fundamentally to rethink the whole problem. This is because of the repercussions that this unemployment among educated young people has had on the economy (social cost of studies and of unemployment, waste of brain-power, etc.), on society and the individual (questioning of traditional values, feeling of uselessness to society, etc.) and sometimes on the political life of each country. It is in this light that the present study, which is focused on unemployment among educated young people in the developed market-economy countries, has been undertaken as one of a series of studies on unemployment among young people in general.

From the outset it must be stressed that this study, of a limited nature, seeks to outline the problems relating to youth unemployment rather than to supply full, structured solutions to these problems. An attempt will first be made to define the meaning of the term 'unemployment'—or at least to indicate the difficulties of supplying such a definition—by relating it to concrete situations of young people with respect to employment (refusal to work, working conditions, types of job remuneration). One of the objectives will be to study further the precise meaning of the various unemployment figures, and then to suggest other methods of approach producing a better definition of the phenomenon, in a wider perspective than its purely numerical aspect.

An analysis will first be made of the characteristic features of youth unemployment—some common to all young people, others unique to educated young people—since this must be the starting point for any attempt at explanation. We must first determine whether there is one type of 'unemployment among young people' or several types. Can young people be classified, as regards work, according to their initial education in school? Are other considerations involved, such as social origin? How can young people's qualifications be defined: with reference to a system of educational values, or to the pattern of employment and the level of remuneration? How do education and qualifications combine to constitute a young person's specific employment situation, for the various levels of education and training?

This method of approach reveals that there is a 'work potential' market[1] where the capability for work of each young person seeking a job is evaluated. In this light, the various employment situations of young people would be merely a reflection of a given labour market structure, in each country and at any given time. As for determining the value assigned to the work potential of each young person, it is not easy to draw up a scale which would allow the problem to be tackled, for example, by taking as a basis the level of training. This cannot be equated simply with a level of education, or a level of professional knowledge and experience. Are there any intrinsic values inherent in each level of education, which determine the value of a given type of work potential? Conversely, is this value always a function of labour market conditions, which are themselves dependent on geographical factors (countries or regions) and on social factors (existence of submarkets for various social and ethnic groups, etc.)?

1. In this study, the expression 'work potential' means all the physical and intellectual abilities of a person which make him or her fit for work.

We must therefore define what constitutes each labour market, as well as the social and economic conditions which determine it. Thus, when a labour market is shrinking generally, does not this phenomenon affect the value of the work potential, i.e. the ability of a young person with a certain level of education to find a job commensurate with that education? On the other hand, when a labour market changes, i.e. when the quality and quantity of vacancies in a certain sector are modified, does not this lead to a general revision of the values assigned to the different levels of knowledge and training? Such quantitative and qualitative changes in the labour market undoubtedly have an influence on the employment situation of young people.

An attempt will be made to unravel the complex relationships which link the evolution of the labour market—i.e. the visible part of the economic and social structures resulting in jobs—with the employment situation facing young people leaving secondary schools and universities, and thus with the value of their work potential. In particular, we must ascertain whether these relationships can be expressed in terms of 'overproduction' of graduates in any one sector or even in general, and this will lead into a discussion of theories concerning the failure of education to adapt to employment patterns.

Having examined some of the consequences of the existence and development of the labour market for the work potential of educated young people, this study will postulate a second hypothesis, namely that the labour market is the result (or end product) at the employment level of the underlying economic and social patterns in a country, as well as of their development. It is through these factors which structure the labour market that the causes of youth unemployment will be sought. This study will consider the rates, the direction and the logic of the growth of market economies, in order then to consider the connections between the labour market and this growth, its direction, and the influence on economic life of power relations at the international level. The study will also come down to the level of the business enterprise, in order to point out some factors concerning the repercussions which the above-mentioned choices have on the organization of work and on working conditions. Within this framework, a description will be given of certain experiments carried out in some countries with a view to integrating the young unemployed person more quickly into working life.

Other programmes or isolated measures are being suggested by governments and non-governmental organizations to solve the problem of youth unemployment. No attempt will be made to draw an exhaustive picture of them, but simply to outline a few approaches to the problem and evaluate the chances of success of these suggestions in the light of their objectives.

Is unemployment among educated young people a separate phenomenon?

The first thing to do when considering the problem of unemployment is to define its scope. This is particularly difficult in the case of young people, for they are on the threshold of their working life, and one must first decide whether they form part of the working population; this seems to be the first criterion which will allow us to define unemployment. Their social situation, and also their family situation—they often still live with their parents and are not heads of families—are objective factors which can affect a definition of the phenomenon.

DEFINING UNEMPLOYMENT

All legal definitions of unemployment, and in particular the international definition given by labour statisticians,[1] assume

1. The definition of unemployment taken from the eighth International Conference of Employment Statisticians, in *Statistiques de Population Active et Inactive*, Geneva, International Labour Office (report No 4, 1954, 64 p.):
   '(a) workers available for employment whose contract of employment has terminated or been temporarily suspended and who are without a job and seeking paid employment;
   (b) persons never previously employed whose most recent status was other than that of employee (i.e. former employers, etc.), together with persons who had been in retirement, who were available for work during the specified period (except for reasons of non-malignant illness) and were seeking paid employment;
   (c) persons without a job and currently available for work who have made arrangements to start a new job at a date subsequent to the specified period;
   (d) persons temporarily or indefinitely laid off without pay.'

that the individual concerned is actually looking for work (except in the case of someone who has been laid off, where reference to that status might seem superfluous). The aim of such definitions is to illustrate and measure an anomaly in the way in which the economy of a country functions. This anomaly will be shown to be the most sharply defined phenomenon to emerge from the imbalance between the population fit for work—even if this is also determined by specific historical and social factors[1]—and the employment opportunities available. If then, in order to be considered as unemployed, one must actually be looking for work, this rules out all cases where an individual wants to work but is not looking for a job (because he has become discouraged or refuses to accept conditions imposed on him) or refuses to work despite having the right age and possessing the desired skills. These situations frequently occur in market economies where work is often fragmented and uninteresting, conditions are unpleasant and pay is inadequate, and where the worker usually has the feeling of hardly participating at all in the life of society, since he is cut off from the places where decisions are taken concerning the organization and content of his working life.[2]

One other aspect is not taken into account in the legal definition of unemployment: the situation of the 'housewife'. It is difficult to imagine that some women 'choose' to stay at home without such a decision being somehow connected with the general conditions to which they are subjected: unequal access to high-grade or responsible posts, and thus to interesting work; unequal pay; lack of accessible social facilities (in particular for their children) which would make their work easier—in short, the whole weight of tradition regarding women's role in the family and in society.

These various situations are often considered to be 'marginal'

1. In particular the age of compulsory schooling and the age of retirement. The demand for labour no doubt also influences in part the length of working life. Other, more subjective, factors are also involved: for example, in the United States only people actually looking for work are counted as members of the working population.
2. See the final report of the 'Symposium of Young Workers on the Quality and Perspectives of Work', Unesco, Paris, 1976.

nd therefore not in the 'unemployment' category. This is
antamount to establishing a norm whereby people are classified
according to their attitude towards the employment which it
seems possible for them to obtain considering the general
conditions of employment. The unemployed, seen in this light,
are those who are willing to look for work in existing conditions: those who are forced to do so by financial or moral
necessity. It must be stressed at once that the fact of looking
for work in the conditions offered by the labour market does
not necessarily mean that one accepts those conditions.[1]

It may already be affirmed that the 'unemployed' category
includes only some of those who, although fit for work, nevertheless do not work for reasons beyond their control: a number
of people who are not looking for a job (and this is the case for
many young people) are in fact deprived of work (and the work
'allergy' of which they are accused is indeed a psychological
phenomenon, but one which is based on a very definite reality:
the fact that the conditions and nature of the work which they
may be offered are incompatible with their aspirations). These
young people, who are no longer at school, who do not work
and who are not considered as 'unemployed', in fact have no
social status. From this viewpoint, the 'unemployed' category
has normative and moral connotations. Those who refuse a job,
or even those who are merely weak-willed and do not follow
up their wish to look for work, are deprived of social status.

This means that the traditional categories,[2] which cannot
evolve because of their rigidity, are incapable of reflecting the
complexities of the present situation and responding to the new
needs. Thus 'marginals' are not included in the 'unemployed'
category, although some of them are certainly 'deprived' of
work, given the conditions described, for political reasons (to
concede that the number of unemployed was increasing would
be equivalent to admitting the failure of a policy), for financial
and economic reasons (the increase would add to the burden of
obligation towards them on the part of the State) and for moral
reasons linked to the other reasons (the status of unemployed

1. This is the position of some left-wing groups which equate refusal to
    work with refusal to accept the conditions of work.
2. Traditional categories: schoolpupil, unemployed, worker, retired, etc.

person, with its 'benefits', cannot be conferred on those who are not looking for work, for this would encourage idleness).

These reasons are sufficient to explain the intentional rigidity of unemployment statistics. In most cases, the inability of statistical indicators to reflect the true state of affairs is considered only from a technical point of view,[1] and comparisons between countries are even more difficult because they do not all use the same indicators.

When other aspects of this insufficiency are considered they are often regarded as phenomena distinct from unemployment, arising out of other problems and therefore needing special solutions. The phenomenon of work refusal and that of the 'housewife', for instance, are seldom analysed as the idealogical results of a specific employment situation and of its connection with the conditions and duration of the time spent 'out of work'.[2]

These phenomena hide the real importance of the need to create jobs. Some phenomena, such as work refusal by young people, being new, lie outside government control. Others however, such as the return of women to the home, can be stimulated by the authorities, which are thus able to keep a pool of labour and relieve congestion on the labour market; but this policy—not a new one—is encountering more and more obstacles because of women's liberation and their wish to work in order to assert their independence, and also because of the need for a second wage to supplement inadequate family incomes. These situations—insufficiency or lack of jobs—should in our opinion be included in any definition of unemployment which is intended to take account of the real need for jobs.

1. See especially: 'Ambiguités des Définitions du Chômage', *Sociologie du Travail* (Paris), July-September 1973, p. 293. This article discusses the relationship between the following categories: population available to look for work, unsatisfied job hunters and labour available to look for work. See also: *Le Chômage des Jeunes et ses Aspects Sociaux*, p. 13-18, Council of Europe, Strasbourg, 1972.
2. In order to explain lack of motivation, mention has been made of the conditions and content of work offered. But we must also take into account the time in a person's life devoted to work (duration, working hours, travelling time) and the difficulty of organizing one's family life while working (lack of social facilities, not enough time at the end of a working day).

Besides actual unemployment, we should point out the problems of underemployment—a term describing the situation of people forced to do part-time work, occasional work or 'inferior' work, i.e. work bearing no relation to their studies or qualifications, or beneath the level of those qualifications. Is underemployment not in fact hidden unemployment? With reference to educated young people, surveys have shown that the first job they have found and taken up seldom corresponds to their aspirations, skills or level of education.[1]

One question arises: how long can such jobs, taken up 'while waiting for something better', last? Underemployment of professional experience and ability acquired through study seems in any case a waste of energy and intelligence, since in this way society forms 'work potentials' for which appropriate employment cannot later be found. This is an important factor which must be taken into account when determining labour requirements. In this connection, two questions arise which will be dealt with later: (a) Are the aspirations of educated young people legitimate? Do they not over-estimate themselves? (b) Is their education of use to the economy of the country? Is there some way of using their qualifications?

To sum up, the legal definitions of unemployment produce a restrictive description of the phenomenon of job requirements, of which they measure only the more visible aspects (excluding underemployment) and the most sharply defined (leaving out the conditions which create situations in which people are out of work but not looking for a job). The objective of these definitions seems to be to define the minimum requirements, below which it is not possible to go without seriously jeopardizing the conservation and renewal of a society's physical and intellectual potential for work.

1. A survey on 'work and society', undertaken in France in 1970 among young people who had just obtained their degrees, showed that four young people out of ten were going to take up posts which they considered as the beginning of a lasting career; 60 per cent had therefore not immediately found work fulfilling this requirement. In 1975, five years later, a third of these young graduates felt that the job they were doing bore no relation to their training, and 11 per cent did not have, or no longer had, any job. For further details see *L'Insertion des Jeunes Diplômés de l'Enseignement Superieur dans la Vie Active,* Paris, Association pour l'Emploi des Cadres (APEC), December 1975.

On the other hand, a definition of unemployment more appropriate to real job requirements, aimed at measuring them exactly with a view to making full use of all society's physical and intellectual capacities, would correspond to the idea of job requirements in a social sense, and would encompass all the people who today make up a vast reserve labour force while still not being unemployed in the eyes of the law.

GENERAL CHARACTERISTICS OF YOUTH UNEMPLOYMENT

In the introduction, the theory was advanced that there is such a thing as a labour market—that is, a place where work potentials[1] are bought and sold. This mechanism requires that work potentials be measured by a suitable scale of values, since they compete on this market. The value assigned to a particular work potential is the result of concrete phenomena which occur on this market: for example, in France professional experience is rated higher than initial training, whereas in the Federal Republic of Germany the reverse is true.[2] It seems that to rate highly certain elements of work potential leads to others being given a low rating because of the climate of competition which reigns on the market, competition which becomes fiercer as the gap widens between job supply and demand. This tendency to give a high or low rating to certain elements—such as training, degrees, experience and also age, sex, family situation, and personality—has certainly not arisen spontaneously. On the contrary, it is the result of the interplay of social criteria, not always explicit, which are invoked in order to give a breakdown of work potential, to classify workers (particularly socially) and to make a selection (since they cannot all be employed).

The criteria determining the value and 'employability' of this work potential are separate from its constituent elements. Thus, it is not the level of training which results in a particular rating, but rather the operational criterion for this training—the

---

1. See definition of this expression in Note 1, page 12.
2. Centre d'Étude des Revenus et des Coûts (CERC); *Structure des Salaires et des Emplois dans les Entreprises Françaises et Allemandes.* Paris, La Documentation Française, 3rd quarter 1974, 60 p.

Table 1. Average length of time spent looking for a job

| Age Group | Number of months | |
	Men	Women
Under 18	3.5	3.1
18-24	3.5	4.2
25-39	4.9	5.1
40-49	4.9	6.9
50 and over	9.5	9.5
Average	4.5	4.9

Source: Cahiers de l'INSEE, p. 52, Paris, 1968.

ability to fill a given job more quickly—which determines the social value of such training on the market. The same seems to be true of all the constituent elements of work potential: they are classed according to this essential criterion of being operational. The sooner a work potential becomes productive, the more employable it is.

This would explain why young people are both more and less employable than other categories of worker. They are more employable because, as shown in Table 1, they remain jobless for less time than the other age groups;[1] in addition, they quickly adapt to a job—precisely because of their youth—and paradoxically their lack of professional experience often leads to their being preferred, lower salaries being the justification; finally, they are more available, having fewer external ties (family and geographical), which on the other hand makes it easier to dismiss them.

Yet more of them than of other age groups (Table 2) are unemployed and the percentage of young people is higher

1. 'In 1973, the time spent looking for a job was under one month for 40 per cent of young graduates, from 2 to 3 months for 40 per cent of them, but less than 1 per cent waited more than 6 months'. ('Les Jeunes et le Travail', *Informations Sociales,* p. 45, Paris, Caisse Nationale d'Allocations Familiales, March 1976.)

Table 2. Unemployment rates of the working population in France (in percentages)

Age Group	Men	Women	Both
Under 18	9.9	23.0	14.9
18-24	6.4	9.3	7.8
25-39	2.0	4.8	3.0
40-49	2.0	4.0	2.7
50-59	2.0	3.4	2.5
60 and over	2.4	2.3	2.3
Average	2.7	5.4	3.8

Source: B. Seys, 'Le Chômage d'Après l'Enquête"Emploi" d'Avril 1975'; *Économie et Statistique,* Paris, Institut National de la Statistique et des Études Économiques (INSEE), No 73, December 1975, 70p.

Table 3. Percentages of unemployed and employed youths of working population in some European countries

Country	Young jobless	Young employed
Austria	36.2	26.9
France	39	19.7
Greece	37.8	20.4
Italy	57.0	18.9
Norway	32.1	30.8

Source: Le Chômage des Jeunes et ses Aspects Sociaux, p. 17, Strasbourg, Council of Europe, 1972.

among the unemployed as a whole than among the whole working population (Table 3). The principal argument serving to 'justify' this situation is again—but the other way round— professional experience: it is expensive to teach a young person a job and it is more directly profitable to engage someone who already has this experience. Sometimes, also, employers claim that young people are less conscientious than their elders and more demanding; but such a view seems somewhat subjective, and too easily advanced by someone who wants to avoid paying the costs of an apprenticeship and is unwilling to create new posts. Other elements are also responsible for the low rating given to the work potential of young people, in particular the obligation to perform military service for young men, and the 'risk' of maternity for young women.

Even among young people themselves, discrimination plays a part, in particular as between boys and girls, qualified and unqualified and also within the subgroup of qualified young people, according to the type of training received. But does this mean that, because one can distinguish between several subgroups in the labour market, there are several 'submarkets' for occupations? That would imply that only certain occupations, forming a submarket, can or must correspond to each level or type of training. In fact, the converse seems closer to the truth: the labour market itself, as a function of the conditions which create it, diversifies itself in order to assign to a particular type of training a value which gives access to a particular occupation. The development of the tertiary sector in all the advanced countries during the 1960s, created a great demand for employees—in particular—who were not required to have completed their secondary education, since the possession of a certificate seemed unnecessary considering the nature of the work to be done.

Today things are quite different: although the technical conditions for the employee's work have not evolved in the direction of more skilled work calling for a higher level of training, that is nevertheless what is now required. We are witnessing a devaluation of the work potential of those who have not obtained a secondary school certificate, and even of those who have, for they cannot now hope to obtain jobs which are more skilled or carry greater responsibility. This increasing demand for qualifications has arisen in response both to the generally higher educational level of young people and to a slowing down in the growth of the tertiary sector and therefore a decrease in the number of jobs available.

It is not therefore the level of education which leads to a particular type of job, but rather the conditions on the labour market which, by making work potentials compete with each

other, assign a higher or lower value to a particular educational
level. Thus, a few years ago, young people in industrialized
capitalist countries were already widely affected by unemploy
ment, but the most hard-hit were those who had left school
early and had not had any vocational training; today all cate
gories of young people are affected, young graduates equally
so. For the latter, it is not only a question of unemployment
but also a devaluation of their work potential.

UNEMPLOYMENT AMONG EDUCATED YOUNG PEOPLE

Can we divide young people into educated and uneducated, and
is there any point in doing so? The question is posed in these
terms because the classic explanation for unemployment among
young people is their lack of training or the inability of training
to adapt to the requirements of employment: those who have
least education are said to be the most disadvantaged with
regard to employment and the most vulnerable to unemployment. Yet one cannot equate educational level with vocational
training.

Is a young person leaving school after or during a normal
secondary education better trained than one who has been only
to primary school? In so far as general culture is concerned, of
course he is better trained, but not as regards employment.
Neither person has had vocational training, but the grade of job,
the type of occupation to which they can aspire, are not the
same. The level of schooling does not correspond to vocational
training in the strict sense of the word; it acts as an instrument
of selection giving access to higher-grade occupations, the grade
being defined as a function of the use made of different types
of knowledge, the diversity and complexity of the work done,
and the degree of initiative and personal responsibility entailed.
We can relate access to higher-grade jobs with social advancement. Nevertheless, educational level is not merely an instrument
of social advancement, since the grade of an occupation and its
level on the social scale are not necessarily identical.

Does the general raising of the educational level not bring
with it a systematic devaluation of that level? This question has
already been answered: for any one occupation, higher and
higher qualifications are required, so that those who had

reached the level previously required now have to be content with lower-grade work.[1] This phenomenon shifts the demarcation line between educated and uneducated young people. What criteria can be used to distinguish between them? The average level of education for one generation? The school leaving age? We can adopt these criteria, but what seems more fundamental is the relation between educational level and the way in which jobs are graded. This relation is determined only partly by the school leaving age or by the average educational level. Very often, young people who have continued their studies beyond the compulsory age limit may find themselves downgraded, because of the low grade of job they are offered, and classified among the young uneducated. We shall draw an arbitrary line at the end of secondary education; this will allow us to analyse the unemployment phenomenon not among 'educated young people' but among the 'most highly educated', whom for convenience we shall call 'young graduates'. It is they who theoretically aspire to the best jobs and who should, according to traditional thinking, be the least in danger of being unemployed.[2] Today the facts are at variance with this theory. Unemployment among young graduates, although a new phenomenon, is growing rapidly.

It is clearly important to measure the extent of youth unemployment, which cannot be done within the restricted framework of this study. Stated simply, several indicators show that this unemployment has in general increased in the European Economic Community (EEC) countries and the United States, both in absolute numbers and apparently, as a percentage of total unemployed (Table 4). This means that

1. This is stressed in an article on unemployment in the Federal Republic of Germany: 'More and more graduates, whose numbers have increased rapidly, are supplanting those with a certificate of secondary education in categories of jobs and vocational training posts which should belong to the school-leavers.' ('Quelques Coûts Sociaux du Deuxième Miracle Allemand', *Problèmes Économiques*, No. 1440, October 1975, p. 17-18.)
2. 'Longer studies lessen the likelihood of unemployment . . . . The longer schooling has lasted, the easier it is to obtain vocational training.' (*Le Chômage des Jeunes et ses Aspects Sociaux*, p. 22, Strasbourg, Council of Europe, 1972.)

Table 4. Percentage of young people among total unemployed

	1969	End of 1975
Belgium (under 25)	10.9	For the EEC as a whole:
France (under 25)	19.6	28 per cent
Sweden (under 25)	11.5	(1.5 million young people
Italy (under 25)	18.9	out of
Netherlands (15-24)	24.5	5.3 million unemployed)
United Kingdom (15-18)	3.8	

Sources: Le Chômage des Jeunes et ses Aspects Sociaux, Strasbourg, Council of Europe, 1972. 'Perspectives Économiques de l'Organisation de Coopération et de Développement Économique' (OCDE), *Liaisons Sociales,* (Paris), No. 85/76, 10 September 1976.

the increase in unemployment affects young people more than it does other categories. On the other hand, there are no statistics showing the extent of unemployment among educated young people, and it would be interesting to measure whether this category is growing faster than that of unemployed young people in general. This seems to be the picture which emerges from various articles and publications, even though no overall study has been made. The country most affected by this phenomenon is the United States,[1] but unemployment is more

1. On the basis of a study of the labour market made by Herbert Bienstock, head of the Bureau of Labor Statistics of New York, Hans Jugersen writes, in the article 'Katzenjammer nach dem Rüstungsboom' *(Frankfurter Allgemeine Zeitung* (Frankfurt), 22 January 1972): 'The present situation on the labour market for chemists and physicists has the immediate result of causing a decrease in enrolments in the universities concerned, which would not in itself be very dramatic if the other branches of higher education could offer better employment prospects. But this is not the case.' Thus, in 1972, out of 5 million unemployed, about 25 per cent were aged between 16 and 19, and somewhat less than 50 per cent were aged between 16 and 24. The same author also points out the considerable increase in the number of unemployed engineers and technicians (for engineers it amounts to 5 per cent of that professional group, or about 70,000 people). These figures suggest considerable unemployment among young graduates.

widespread in some other countries which have not yet reached
the level of the United States, as shown in Table 5.

It will be noted that it is those countries where unemployment is still least widespread (Denmark, Federal Republic of
Germany, France) which have the fastest rate of increase in
unemployment. Can we assume from this that unemployment
will gradually affect the young graduate category in all these
countries? What analysis can be made of the employment
situation of these young graduates? Recent surveys[1] have
shown the difficulties they have in finding work. Very few, on
leaving college, land a post bearing any relation to the course
they have followed, or one which they 'consider to be the start
of a permanent career'. Faced with these difficulties, some
continue their studies in order to obtain a second degree, a
second specialization, hoping in this way to improve their
chances of finding a job. In fact, they only delay their entry
on the job market, for most of them do not obtain a higher

Table 5. Overall unemployment and its rate of increase

	Percentage of working population	Increase in one year (1974-75)
Federal Republic of Germany	3.86	+110.9
Belgium	4.92	+ 73.6
Denmark	3.07	+149.8
France	3.46	+ 92.3
Italy	5.54	+ 14.7
Netherlands	4.42	+ 57.6
United Kingdom	4.25	+ 80.9
United States	8.82	+ 56.1

Source: J. P. Revoil, 'Evolution de l'Emploi en 1974 et au Début de
1975', *Economie et Statistique* (Paris), No. 69, July/August 1975.

---

1. Centre d'Etudes et de Recherches sur les Qualifications (CEREQ),
   *Accès à la Vie Professionnelle: Enseignement Technique Technolo-
   gique Long, Second Cycle*, Paris, La Documentation Française, January
   1973, 160 p.

degree.[1] This phenomenon, which is on the increase accentuates inequality of opportunity in employment as a resul of the social origin of young people; those from humble back grounds, of whom only a small minority receive post-secondar education, have even more difficulty in thus continuing thei studies. The inflation and accumulation of degrees, whicl reflect narrowing opportunities and competition between youn people and other workers on the labour market, aggravate socia inequality as concerns employment.

All young graduates are not therefore in the same positior as regards finding jobs. There is a close connection betweer social background, the post-secondary stream (or branch o education) chosen and the chances of finding the right jol quickly. The universities or colleges which are most highly 'rated' on the labour market are also those which admit the smallest number of young people from poorer families, because of the difficulty of gaining admission to them as well as the cos and length of studies. Nevertheless, even these colleges also 'turn out' unemployed graduates, who paradoxically take longer to find work than other people; obviously because of their own expectations based on their level of education, they have great difficulty in accepting more humble jobs. It is noteworthy that these young people, who are—or should be—the most highly prized on the labour market, also find that their work potential is devalued when they accept low-grade jobs and when they are unemployed, for then their work potential is neither utilized nor properly remunerated.

The lower we go on the scale of values for degrees obtained (one or two degrees, one science or arts degree, etc.), the more widespread we can assume unemployment to be, and the more the jobs accepted reflect a devaluation of acquired skills. As was shown in the survey made by APEC in 1975, 37 per cent of a group of young graduates, five years after obtaining their degree, had not yet found permanent employment which had

---

1. Centre d'Études et de Recherches sur les Qualifications (CEREQ): *Les Possibilités d'Emploi selon les Qualifications Acquises dans les Formations Initiales*, Paris, Ministère de l'Education Nationale, Office National d'Information sur les Enseignements et les Professions, La Documentation Française, June 1972, 147 p.

any bearing on their course of study. They were mostly young
people from poor families, who had been to university and who,
during the period surveyed, had had to take a variety of jobs,
usually requiring no qualifications.

To sum up, there is an observable trend towards the
lengthening of the study period and the accumulation of
degrees, coupled with increasing unemployment among young
graduates, more occupational mobility and the growing and
lasting acceptance of low-grade jobs. All these phenomena help
to devalue the work potential of young graduates, especially
those from lower-class families. The prolonging of student life
and the pursuit of degrees, which result from the scarcity of
employment opportunities, contribute in their turn to the
inflation and devaluation of degrees; but these two phenomena
are not the basic cause, as will be seen in the next chapter.

Unemployment is the most severe form of work potential
devaluation, because then the potential is unused and unpaid.
Only for a small minority of unemployed people do unemployment benefits amount to as much as a wage, and most of the
time the benefits are not even enough to pay for food and
lodging. As for the young unemployed, many of them get
nothing at all. Occupational mobility and low-grade jobs often
go together, this mobility reflecting refusal to accept a job
deemed inferior in relation to the degree held, on the basis of
what that degree was previously worth on the labour market.

But the more this state of affairs spreads, the more unemployment increases and the acceptance of low-grade jobs
grows, finally becoming the norm for a given level of study or
degree. This process leads to a permanent, not temporary,
devaluation of work potential, a devaluation which produces
a chain reaction: since young graduates are now taking jobs
which previously went to primary or secondary school-leavers,
the latter fall back on the lowest-grade jobs or are forced into
unemployment. Unemployment among educated and uneducated young people in fact plays a similar part in this process:
it acts as a means of bringing economic pressure to bear on
young people (principally, but also on other workers) so that
they accept tasks which are less and less commensurate with
their studies, their training and their physical and intellectual
ability. In this sense, unemployment is an instrument of de-

valuation of the overall work potential. The law of supply
and demand is a factor in this devaluation, but the relationship
between the number of job hunters (actual or potential) and the
number of jobs available is not the only element which
influences this process.

We have alluded to the 'qualification' aspect of this relation
stressing that the educational level of workers and the type of
training they have received—especially for young people arriving
on the labour market—are not unimportant when one analyses
the phenomenon whereby a decreasing value is assigned to a
particular physical or intellectual ability to work. The causes of
this devaluation and of unemployment among educated young
people will now be examined.

Causes of unemployment among educated young people

If the problem is stated in terms of the relationship between job supply and demand, the first questions about the causes of unemployment among educated young people are: Are there too many young graduates for the needs of the economy? And are they being misdirected in view of these needs? All studies on the subject answer these questions in the affirmative, and conclude that the educational system is ill-adapted to working life. This is the basic cause of unemployment among young people, including educated young people.

EDUCATION AND EMPLOYMENT

No educational system has ever been free of shortcomings. But previously these shortcomings did not give rise to unemployment. Have they become bad enough to reach a point where young people are so ill-prepared for working life that they can only be unemployed?

Lack of adaptability and selection

Education has always been, and still is, cut off from life. School curricula are always designed to provide 'general education' with a literary bias, bearing no relation to the discoveries and present-day use of science and technology. Social and economic life is still largely ignored in this basic education, although some progress has been made in this regard. Young pupils must specialize earlier and earlier in a particular branch of knowledge; thus prevented from having an overall view of modern knowledge and narrowly confined, they have difficulty in grasping the realities of modern life, and even in relating what they learn to the social and economic life of the country.

The growing compartmentalization of education prefigures the division of the tasks that young people will be called upon to perform in their future occupations. At school, children already lose (or do not acquire) the ability to find their place in the life of society, to understand that they bear a measure of responsibility in its progress. The content and structure of education help to hide from them the real role they will play in production, so that they lose interest in their future job and their present school work, for they are less and less able to see its usefulness to society and they are well aware that the share of responsibility falling to them will be ever smaller.

While the educational system has never given young people an overall view of the society in which they were to live and work, it nevertheless allowed them a certain social advancement which was enough to motivate them in respect of their studies. (However, we must stress that social advancement has never meant awareness of one's responsibility in the life of the country.) Lengthy studies and degrees are less and less able to ensure this social advancement. They no longer automatically give access to responsible posts and top-grade jobs, whereas in the past the educational system made a social selection that was sufficient to fill posts of this type, which were relatively few.

Two factors combined to produce this result. The post-war rapid industrial progress, the emergence of new technologies (computers and automation) and the growth of the tertiary sector created many new jobs, in particular for executives, technicians and research workers. Degrees were much in demand: studies of the American market at that time even stress the shortage of executives in certain areas of activity. At the same time, the educational system was more severe in its social selection than it is today, and allowed only a limited number of young people to reach the post-secondary level. They were therefore sure of finding employment at the end of their course of study. Faced with this need for graduates, governments then placed more emphasis on education and lengthened schooling. Today, these privileged young people are more numerous, but they are no longer privileged: the economic recession in all the developed countries means that they can no longer fit all the young graduates into jobs which match their qualifications. This loss of 'social effectiveness' among graduates spotlights the irrelevance of education and its failure to adapt to life. As M. Freyssenet emphasizes:

Although secondary and higher education was tedious, unsuitable and sometimes perfunctory, it was accepted and tolerated so long as it was truly socially effective—so long as it gave effective access to an appropriate level of employment, and so long as the social function to which it led was not devalued. From being tedious, secondary and higher education became pointless as soon as its social effectiveness decreased perceptibly.[1]

This being so, it seems that in the market-economy countries education has never been purposely designed as a preparation for working life, but rather as an instrument of selection for channelling young people towards a hierarchy of occupations by maintaining social inequality as regards access to these occupations. Thus social categories were perpetuated from generation to generation. We cannot therefore invoke the lack of adaptability of education in order to justify or explain unemployment among educated young people.

Having stated this conclusion, we may stress that, in the present context of employment crisis, failure to adapt education is what most hampers young people in search of a job; it does so in different ways, however, according to the educational stream they have followed.

Technical and scientific education

Early specialization which is becoming more and more common in many educational systems is a response to the requirements voiced by employers who want a more narrowly specialized labour force corresponding to the technologies for each branch of activity. Governments were therefore concerned to adapt the content of education to the new social division of labour and the new technologies, but only at a minimal cost and without giving young people a broadly-based general education. Specialization starts very early, and its nature is such that it smacks more of learning how to follow instructions and directions for

1. M. Freyssenet, *Le Processus de Déqualification—Surqualification de la Force de Travail*, p. 233-4, Paris, Centre de Sociologie Urbaine, 1974.

use than of grasping the basic theories underlying those instructions.

Such training met the short-term needs of the economy so long as it was expanding and offered broad openings for each branch of education. But today, with the economic recession and the employment crisis, it has become a definite handicap. Young people, not finding work in the narrow field for which they have been trained, have difficulty being accepted on the labour market for other jobs requiring an equivalent level of qualification. The marked division of labour and young people's lack of a sufficiently general theoretical training does not make it easy for them to retrain. In addition, employers find that such retraining is too costly and does not produce immediate returns. In view of the competition on the labour market, they prefer to engage experienced workers rather than young graduates. Not finding it easy to retrain, these young people are the victims of the law of immediate returns, both on the labour market and during their education. Most affected are graduates from the technical and scientific streams. Indeed, in those areas, unemployment affects not only young people but all workers.

This shows that, while many young people are out of work, it is not because education is ill-adapted to the needs of the economy; that merely makes young people more vulnerable to unemployment than other categories of worker. In fact, the adaptation of education to provide greater specialization and not more profound general culture met the short-term needs of the economy during a phase of expansion and intensification of the division of labour. But today this trend is a source of difficulty for the same economy: what society was unwilling to spend at the educational stage, it will now have to pay out in unemployment benefits and sometimes in the cost of retraining; but retraining, far from being a broad, general education which would give access to a diversity of jobs, will consist of the acquisition of a new specialization, which will only postpone the problem.

Liberal arts education

As for so-called liberal arts education, it has different characteristics. Far more remote from working life, it represented the

tream of 'social advancement' *par excellence*. Degrees in liberal
arts, together with a general school certificate, were a means of
social selection and traditionally gave access to responsible posts
n teaching, research and the higher realms of the public
sector.[1] In the private sector, they have been supplanted by
business and science degrees, which are more highly specialized
and directly profitable. In so far as the recession affects all these
sectors, these degrees have lost their 'social advancement'
function, and the rigid nature of such an education is clearly
apparent, although it is not the cause of the unemployment of
its young ex-students. Nor can one blame this unemployment
on poor distribution or the misdirecting of young people as
regards the various types of education. As has been seen, other
young business or science graduates also have trouble finding
work.

The problem of unemployment among educated young
people therefore arises in all categories of education, even
though liberal arts education is affected more than the others.
In absolute terms, liberal arts degrees have certainly undergone
a devaluation on the labour market, for several reasons: above
all, because on this market the holders of liberal arts degrees
find themselves competing with each other and with other
workers; and this competition is intensified when the number of
high-grade occupations does not increase at the same rate as the
number of newly-qualified workers and graduates. In addition,
scientific and technical degrees have gained in value on the
labour market since they make the young worker more rapidly
profitable, part of his training having been given to him during
his education, paid for out of public funds or by himself, not by
the employer. It must also be noted that very many jobs today
require a much higher level of technical and scientific knowledge
than was formerly the case and that the 'training required'
indicated in job advertisements is explicitly and clearly defined
for each post by the employers. This is done with utilitarian
intentions, deliberately ignoring the candidates' general educa-

. Centre d'Études et de Recherches sur les Qualifications, *Accès à la Vie Professionnelle*, op. cit.

tion.[1] Finally, career opportunities for liberal arts graduates (in administration, teaching, research, etc.) depend largely on public funds, and it seems that the options and budgetary obligations of governments and public bodies have resulted in a gradual devaluation of these jobs (particularly in administration) as compared with similar jobs in the private sector.

Selection in education has adapted to these economic facts this has resulted in the formation of an élite in high-level technical and scientific fields; other students are then relegated to arts courses and their degrees thus become less highly rated. In addition to this selection there is one which operates between universities at different levels, so those to which it is easiest to gain entry find that the market value of their degrees is declining. And all these processes, which tend to offset the movement towards more democratic education, are mutually reinforcing.[2]

New needs and factors tending to repress these needs

The general devaluation of degrees has very little to do with a decrease in the real worth, in working life, of the learning which they represent. Rather, it is a reduction in the effectiveness of degrees in respect of their immediate profitability, because of the narrowing of the labour market which necessitates an increasing degree of selection starting at the educational stage.[3] Education adapts to working life above all through selection, of which the separation of students into different groups is a part.

1. However, general education is often a factor when applicants are selected for certain jobs, and it often bears a direct relationship to the social background of the candidate. Many surveys have in fact shown the relationship which exists between social background and the possibility of attaining a certain cultural level.
2. New York University, which used to be the only American university where courses of study were free, recently began to charge tuition fees; for this reason, a large number of young people from poor families can no longer continue their higher education there.
3. New needs are becoming apparent, in particular because of the efforts being made to enrich cultural life; they may result in the creation of good jobs for liberal arts graduates, but these jobs are not 'profitable'.

The content of study courses is evolving principally as a result of the introduction of different systems of education allowing the separation of students according to the type of course followed (long courses, technical studies, etc.). The present inadaptation of education, which is of concern to governments, is said by some to be due to an excessive democratization of studies (but in a limited sense, because the social patterns in the student population is still the reverse image of that of society as a whole); in other words, too many graduates are being produced at a time of economic recession. But such an opinion seems to owe too much to Malthusian ideas. Far from promoting the advancement of science and technology, limiting the number of graduates would only increase still further the number of jobs which have been down-graded and the number of unemployed people, or else make occupations less skilled by reducing the period of study of those who will perform them. (This is particularly true of teachers in France, whose professional training is quite inadequate.) The most obvious result of all the steps taken to adapt education to present employment requirements is that the development of education is being slowed down for large sections of society.

The principal arguments put forward in support of these steps are economic; but they take the short view, for the country's general growth calls on the contrary for the growth of knowledge in all fields and the sharing of this knowledge in society. However, social and political motives are also involved. The democratization of education can become 'subversive', for it gives rise to new demands; in spite of its shortcomings, education does open the minds of young people to the world and its history and, by giving a new outlook, it creates needs. The young person now wants a job which is interesting, which calls on his powers of thought and of creation; he also wants access to a richer cultural and social life. When these needs spread into social strata other than the ruling 'élite', the latter becomes alarmed, for it can no longer consider education merely as an instrument of social integration. A certain democratization of education was necessitated by growth, but the economic crisis today is reversing this trend and accentuating the contrast between young people's desire to learn, to think and to create and the opportunities which they have for doing so

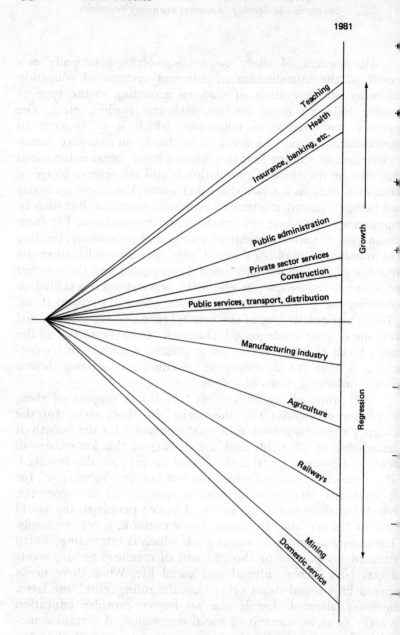

Fig. 1. United Kingdom: Compound annual rate of growth or regression in 1981. *(From: Department of Employment Gazette, London, May 1975.)*

in their educational career and their working life. So, in order to stem the dissatisfaction which this situation necessarily arouses, a whole panoply of measures and ideas is being used to repress the new needs. Efforts are being made to discourage young people from taking long courses by erecting numerous selection barriers (including financial ones) and by spreading the idea that their efforts will not give them a creative and well-paid job. The growing division of labour and the down-grading of jobs combine to divert young people from courses leading to such prospects. Finally, these form the foundations for the phenomenon of the return to nature and to craftsmanship, which reflects the refusal of the individual to accept conditions of work and the alienation which they engender.

In reality, man is not benefiting from technological progress and scientific development; these are being used only to increase the productivity of labour, which seems irreconcilable with improved working conditions and a reduction in the divorce between manual and intellectual work, between routine and creative activity.

THE LABOUR MARKET: RECESSION AND DEVALUATION

The economic recession: its effects on employment

An analysis of the visible manifestations of the economic recessions—which involves all industrialized market-economy countries—shows that low-grade jobs (and primarily those in industry) have been and still are the ones most affected by the crisis, but also that unemployment does not spare the tertiary sector, on the one hand, and managerial and scientific jobs on the other. In these circumstances, young people are obviously the first to fall by the wayside, especially since their unemployment costs the least. This recession, which first affected the productive sectors (see Fig. 1) and particularly agriculture and traditional industries (mining, foodstuffs, textiles, etc), is today reaching the industries using advanced technology. In France, the recession, which began in agriculture and industry, has gradually spread to all sectors, as shown in Table 6.

40   *Simone Morio*

Table 6. Average annual growth of employment in France

Sectors	1960-65	1965-70	1970-73	1973-88[1] I	II
Agriculture	− 3.7	− 3.8	− 4.2	− 3.8	− 3.8
Agricultural and foodstuffs industries	− 0.1	− 0.3	− 0.5	− 0.5	− 0.1
Energy	− 0.5	− 1.6	− 1.5	− 4.5	− 4.8
Industry	1.3	0.6	1.3	0.5	0.2
Transport and telecommunications	2.2	1.1	0.9	0.4	0.3
Housing	1.2	3.1	2.9	0.8	0.8
Construction and public works	4.1	1.4	0.1	− 0.4	− 0.9
Services	2.4	4.1	3.4	3.0	2.4
Business	1.9	2.0	1.7	1.6	1.0
Civil service, banking, insurance	2.8	2.6	2.6	2.3	2.3

1. Projections based on two hypotheses.

Source: Comité Emploi et Travail, Commissariat Général au Plan, *Emploi et Travail, Préparation due VIIe Plan*, Table 23, p. 72, Paris, La Documentation Française, 1976, 400 p.

In the United States,

The elimination of budgetary allocations affects employment not only in administrations or agencies, but above all in all the sectors of supply, at the research level as well as the manufacturing level. Thus the cuts in credits for NASA and the Pentagon have recently resulted in the elimination of nearly two million jobs . . . . many of which were highly skilled. . . . Among the branches most affected are industries connected with the production of aerospace equipment.[1]

Other indicators, such as the GNP and the GDP, show that the

1. 'Le marché du Travail aux Etats-Unis', *Revue économique de la B.N.P.* (Paris), January 1974.

Table 7. Percentage changes in GNP in certain OECD countries

Country	1974	1975
Luxembourg	+ 4.5	− 3
Federal Republic of Germany	+ 0.6	− 1.5
Italy	+ 3.4	− 1.5
Netherlands	+ 1.8	− 1
Belgium	+ 4	0
France	+ 3.8	0
Ireland	+ 0.4	0
Denmark	+ 1.6	+ 0.5
United Kingdom	0	+ 1
United States	− 2.1	− 4
Japan	− 1.8	+ 1

Source: 'Perspectives Économiques de l'OCDE', *Liaisons Sociale* (Paris) p. 3, 19 August 1975 (Document No. 63/75).

recession has hit practically every OECD country (Table 7). However, these indicators do not reflect the number of jobs created. Thus in 1976 a slight improvement in GNP was noted, but unemployment stayed the same, and even worsened. Why? First of all, this recovery was very modest, and by the end of 1976 the level of production in the OECD countries had not yet reached the 1973 level; above all, it resulted in the creation of only very few jobs. We shall see the reasons for this further on (Table 8).

The manufacturing sector as an instrument of growth

Recovery goes hand in hand with the concentration of industry, beginning with the manufacturing sector. It has been observed that, when the number of jobs in this sector decreases, unemployment increases and that this phenomenon has repercussions shortly afterwards in the non-manufacturing sector. For example, in France the period 1955-61 was characterized by considerable growth in industrial jobs and a drop in unemployment; on the other hand, the period 1965-67 saw an increase in the number of jobs in the tertiary sector, but unemployment

Table 8. Percentage changes in employment in selected professional and managerial occupations

Profession	1950-60	1960-70	Projection 1970-80[1]
Teachers, elementary and secondary	+ 48	+ 44	+ 2
University teachers and equivalent	+ 43	+ 138	+ 48
Scientists	+ 28	+ 65	+ 38
Engineers	+ 63	+ 38	+ 35
Physicians	+ 27	+ 25	+ 42
Dentists	+ 28	+ 10	+ 30
Professional nurses	+ 42	+ 38	+ 39
Social scientists	+ 60	+ 125	+ 38
Accountants and auditors	+ 25	+ 55	+ 35
Lawyers and judges	+ 22	+ 38	+ 20
Company managers	+ 45	?	+ 70
Company presidents and directors	− 21	− 39	?

1. The projections shown in the right-hand column were calculated in 1970; however, at that date, although the economic recession had not reached the low of 1976, many socio-professional categories were already in decline.

Source: M. S. Gordon: *Higher Education and the Labor Market*, New York, 1974, 630 p.

also rose.[1] Today, the number of jobs in the tertiary sector is not growing. This sector recruits mainly from the reserve labour force (women especially), whereas industry takes its recruits from all categories of job hunter. This explains to a certain extent how there can be an increase in tertiary sector jobs and yet a rise in unemployment. The nucleus of unemployment is

1. Salais and Eymard-Duvernay, 'Les Relations Complexes entre les Créations d'Emplois et l'évolution du Chômage en France', *Problèmes Économiques* (Paris), No. 1419, 23 April 1975, p. 14-19.

in the manufacturing industry, and the artificial creation of jobs in administration or the service industries is only a short-term palliative for unemployment and cannot absorb it completely. Hence the repeated appeals by international organizations for governments to create jobs for young people, particularly in administration, has had only a slight effect on youth unemployment.

In order to cause a real drop in unemployment, economic growth must first affect manufacturing industry, and be accompanied by a deliberate policy of job creation in this sector. [1] When the number of jobs in the non-manufacturing sector increases while there is a stand-still or a drop in jobs in the manufacturing industry, the latter, which is the only producer of wealth, is forced to bear an ever-increasing social cost. Since the wealth created is not limitless, and its production decreases during a period of economic recession, it becomes impossible to finance the growth of the non-manufacturing sector where, on the contrary, the number of jobs begins to decline. A certain balance must therefore be maintained, based on the productivity of the moment, between the number of manufacturing jobs and number of non-manufacturing jobs so as not to restrict growth, the resorption of unemployment being a basic element of such growth. Determined measures taken by certain governments with a view to providing jobs for young people, or directing them towards vocational training, are nothing more than a switching of resources which momentarily supports one sector in a state of crisis while weakening another, without providing a fundamental solution to the problem of unemployment.

The restructuring of companies

Restructuring is often put forward as an explanation of unemployment. How does it work? Is it inevitable?

The economic depression has speeded up the process of

---

1. Some governments have understood this need. In France, for instance, a campaign has been launched to upgrade manual work; but this campaign remains still very theoretical, for it has not been accompanied by specific measures to ensure the creation of jobs and the improvement of working conditions.

concentration, of takeovers, of mergers among companies. The big firms have passed on to their subcontractors the difficulties encountered on the market, and a large number of the latter have had to lay off workers or put them on part time, or even go into liquidation. All these operations combine to result in a decrease in the number of jobs or in working hours. The redistribution of major investments among the various branches of activity seems to reflect not the logic behind the country's economic structure but rather the power relationship between capital at the international level. There are many inconsistencies in the policy of restructuring businesses. A country may abandon one area of production, thereby becoming forced to import the goods concerned; another may halt research in a certain field, thus jeopardizing its technological progress and lead in the market. This phenomenon can be explained only by reference to the keen competition for world markets between major companies. These markets being limited—especially as a large proportion of the population is unemployed—the ascendancy of one group means that it is impossible for other firms to survive on this market.

For the workers, this restructuring leads inevitably to unemployment. Can governments, in these circumstances, erect barriers to protect workers in their countries? They would have to re-examine the competition between monopolies, at the risk of depriving their national enterprises of the export markets where they make much of their profit. This would upset the whole system. Certain governments, such as the Netherlands Government, have attempted measures designed to redirect a dying industry towards another branch of activity; but these attempts could be neither prolonged nor widespread. While they maintained the level of employment, they would have been financially profitable only in the long term—a delay which is unacceptable to industry and to financiers. As was emphasized in an article in an American magazine: 'Investors want a good deal more: they want to be able to get their money out in three years, they want very high interest rates, and they want control of the company.'[1]

1.   'Making U.S. Technology more Competitive', *Business Week* (New York), 15 January 1972.

It is difficult to reconcile these requirements with planned industrial investment designed to solve the problem of unemployment and ensure the best use of national wealth. Monopolistic restructuring leads not to rational employment of this wealth but to an increasingly marked division of labour at the international level, which is sometimes detrimental to the country's most precious commodity. Such restructuring, which is therefore incompatible with the logic of the country's economic and social structure, is one of the basic causes of the difficulties experienced by young graduates in finding work, since all levels of occupation are affected by the unemployment caused by this restructuring.

Job structure

Adding to the problems caused by the concentration of industry, the introduction of new technologies is also instrumental in reducing the number of workers and down-grading a large number of occupations. By increasing labour productivity, automation reduces the amount of labour required, except where the expansion of a company makes it possible to offset lay-offs by recruiting more workers (but at the expense of other firms which have been ousted from the market). Automation causes a large number of jobs to be down-graded, and calls for an increased degree of skill in only a minority of jobs. In short, there are fewer high-grade jobs than before, and therefore fewer openings for young graduates looking for work. The consequences of this down-grading are felt in several ways: the work is less interesting, less use is made of acquired knowledge, and the pay is lower. To recruit young graduates for this type of work is a waste of the knowledge they have acquired and a devaluation of their degrees.

Some people seek to justify this state of affairs by completely eliminating the 'utilitarian' aspect of education, reducing it to a sort of 'cultural luxury', designed not 'to be of use' in one's subsequent working life but simply to enrich the mind.[1] This is an ideological attempt to make young graduates

1.   J. Delors, 'Emploi et Formation: La Conciliation Impossible', *Cahiers Français*, Paris, La Documentation Française, March-April 1976.

accept inferior jobs, but it also underlines the difficulty of retracing one's steps in the face of the present-day demand for learning and the progress achieved in that regard. It is difficult to lower the average standard of education in order to adapt it to the limited and utilitarian needs of the economic system, but it is by no means impossible. It would be sufficient to erect more selection barriers at every level and to stress the risk of being unemployed if one has a degree, or of not using it in one's working life, in order effectively to slow down educational development and to discourage young people of poorer families from pursuing studies.

Is this down-grading of jobs inevitable, and is the introduction of new technologies incompatible with a parallel increase in the number of highly-skilled jobs? We are a long way from finding answers to these questions, but what is certain is that automation is not being introduced with the idea of preserving skilled occupations. On the contrary, profitability of work potential is the only object. This makes for increased productivity by creating lower-grade jobs which are therefore less well paid than were the more numerous jobs, at various levels, which are thus replaced.

However, the shortage of openings for young graduates is not due to the introduction of new technologies alone, if only because these have not yet been introduced on a wide scale into industry and the tertiary sector, and are still pilot experiments in many cases. The distribution of tasks and responsibilities within the business firm also plays a role in this respect. Thus a study by the Centre d'Étude des Revenus et des Coûts (CERC)[1] highlights substantial disparities between the two countries examined, namely France and the Federal Republic of Germany. Salary range, particularly in relation to age, is wider in France and young people have less access to executive and managerial posts. On the other hand, promotion by seniority is more general there, whereas in German companies it is relatively hard to break out of the initial compartments. This does not mean that there are fewer low-grade jobs in the Federal Republic of Germany, but simply that the exploitation of workers extends

---

1.　Centre d'Étude des Revenus et des Coûts, *Structure des Salaires et des Emplois dans les Entreprises Françaises et Allemandes,* op. cit.

ver the whole of their working life and to the entire labour
orce, while in France it is more concentrated at the start of a
areer, and particularly for certain jobs.

A real redistribution of jobs and pay which would give
oung people especially more opportunities to hold responsible
ositions cannot come about by a levelling down and further
ompartmentalization of occupations. It requires a decentral-
zation of responsibility within the company. What we see,
owever, is just the opposite: concentration of essential
lecision-making in the hands of a very small number of top
xecutives, a concentration which is sometimes camouflaged by
seudo-democratic practices (meetings between management
nd employees where everyone gives opinions and advice),
imed at cloaking the real centralization of power and at
reating an illusion of democracy which is in fact purely super-
icial. Attempts have been made, in the Netherlands particularly,
o restructure jobs within companies, but these measures could
ot be continued or expanded because they tended to run
ounter to the goal of making work potential profitable. To ask
. worker to undertake different, and therefore more complex,
asks certainly makes his work more interesting for him; but
his versatility also requires greater skill and therefore higher
ay: so there has again been a growing compartmentalization
f jobs, which has even reached the tertiary sector.

The public sector has not been exemplary in this respect.
Quite the contrary, in some countries the first experiments in
ntroducing computers into non-manufacturing work are taking
lace in the public sector, which thus acts as a testing ground
or the private sector; yet these experiments lead to the down-
,rading of a considerable number of jobs (in France this is the
ase in certain government departments) by necessitating a
igh degree of compartmentalization of work in all categories
f occupation, from those of skilled engineer to manual worker,
ncluding clerical workers.

Research policies

\s with education, governments (and industrialists) pursue a
Malthusian policy with regard to research: they concentrate on
vhat is profitable in the short term and more or less disregard

basic research. On the human plane, the wastage is huge. Thus in the United States

some 3 per cent of U.S. scientists and engineers now are unemployed. This has helped to discourage many youths who ordinarily would have started studying for technical careers, and manpower experts predict future shortages in the technically trained work force. [1]

From the economic viewpoint, this trend is equally serious growth can resume in a lasting way only if it is firmly based on research, and major innovation cannot come about through short-term research. In addition,

These trends add up, in the eyes of many experts, to a slowdown in U.S. technology. The impact of such a slowdown would not be apparent to consumers for several years, but it shows up quickly in industry. And because of the accelerating pace of technology, even a temporary slackening can put a company far behind. [2]

The abandonment of whole areas of basic research is a phenomenon which has not only begun in the United States. All the developed capitalist countries are familiar with this contradiction: to seek the highest profits in the short term is to mortgage the future and jeopardize progress and future profits.

In the foregoing pages an attempt has been made to show that economic recession and the devaluation of work potential explain the development of unemployment, particularly among educated young people. But these phenomena do not arise spontaneously: they are the fruit of economic structures and, in order to understand unemployment, we cannot consider solely the crisis in these structures: we must consider the structures themselves.

ECONOMIC STRUCTURES AND UNEMPLOYMENT

Apart from the theories just mentioned, which blame unemployment on faulty educational and employment planning, there are other theories which explain it by the need to make a choice between inflation and full employment.

1. 'Making U.S. technology more competitive', op cit.
2. Ibid.

Table 9. Evolution of production, prices, unemployment and purchasing power in France, 1968-76 (1964 = 100)

	1968	1970	1972	1974	1975	1976
Growth in volume of GDP	120.5	136.3	151.8	165.5	162	—
General level of prices	113.8	128.6	144.1	172.6	192.9	216.9
Unemployment rate	192.6	156.8	212.3	211.8	—	—
Purchasing power (January, Paris region)	100			97.9	94.3	91.4

Sources: J. C. Vassal, 'La Stagflation, une Analyse de l'Expérience Française 1964-1974', *Problèmes Économiques* (Paris), No. 1457, 28 January 1976, p. 2-8. For purchasing power, see J. Magniadas, 'Les Salariés Victimes de l'Inflation', *Le Peuple,* No. 998, 1 October 1976, pp. 7-10 (publication of the Confédération Générale du Travail).

Inflation and unemployment

According to certain economists, it is not possible both to maintain purchasing power (price stability) and to enjoy full employment, since the investment needed for the latter is inevitably followed by inflation; on the other hand, if this investment is not made, there will indeed be unemployment, but also price stability. This theory is today disproved by experience. We can see that inflation and unemployment have co-existed for some years; moreover, these two ills are today aggravated by a standstill in production and a fall in the purchasing power of workers, as the figures in Table 9 show for France.

To explain inflation as a consequence of the rise in salary costs is incompatible with the fall in purchasing power and the increase in unemployment. We must therefore look for the explanation elsewhere than in the 'vicious circle' of wages and prices. In fact, inflation is not the price paid for full employment. If we look at the figures in Table 10, we can see a common characteristic for all the countries: the continuous—and

Table 10. Economic indicators and unemployment

	Canada	United States	Japan	France	Federal Republic of Germany	Italy	United Kingdom
Growth in volume of GNP or GDP							
Average 1959/60 to 1972/73	5.1	4.2	10.9	5.9	4.9	5.6	3.3
1974	3.2	−1.8	−1.3	3.9	0.4	3.4	−0.1
1975	0.6	−2.0	−2.2	−2.4	−3.4	−3.7	−1.6
1976	5.0	7.0	6.25	6.25	5.50	1.50	−2.25
Increase in retail price index (in per cent compared with previous year)							
Average 1959/60 to 1972/73	2.6	2.6	6.0	4.5	3.3	4.6	4.1
1974	10.6	10.5	24.5	13.7	7.3	19.1	15.6
1975	10.4	7.8	11.9	11.7	6.1	17.0	22.1
1976	8.0	5.25	9.25	10.5	4.75	20.0	16.0
Balance of payments (in $1,000 million)							
1974	−1.7	−0.6	−4.7	−6.0	9.7	−8.0	−8.7
1975	−5.0	11.7	−0.7	0.3	3.7	−0.6	−3.8

Percentage of unemployed in working population

1970	4.9	1.2	1.7	0.6	3.2	2.2
1973	4.9	1.3	2.1	1.0	3.5	2.3
1974	7.4	1.4	2.3	2.3	5.3	2.8
February 1975	8.9	2.0	3.5	4.5	5.6	3.1
February 1976	8.5	...	4.5	5.1	...	5.1

Sources: 'Perspectives Économiques des L'OCDE', *Liaisons Sociales*, p. 4, Document 85/76, 10 September 1976; 'Le Chômage dans les Pays Industrialisés, *Intersocial*, 9, October 1975, and 15, April 1976 (quoted in *Liaisons Sociales*, Documents 85/75T and 42/76T, Paris, 1975 and 1976).

for most of them, rapid—rise in the rate of unemployment, existing alongside of sustained inflation. In those countries where production and trade have begun to pick up and have even exceeded the average for 1960-72 (United States, France, Federal Republic of Germany), this has not resulted in a reduction in unemployment (except in the United States, but even there only a small reduction). Moreover, inflation does not get production going again, inflation is not the price of growth. In addition, a recovery in production is scarcely ever accompanied by job creation, since it is concomitant with high unemployment rates. The various attempts by governments to create jobs have not had any effect on the great majority of jobless. What attempts have been made, and why did they fail?

Government measures and proposals to combat unemployment.

Bonuses for the creation of jobs (especially for young people) and employment subsidies.

This type of measure is based on the principle that it is better to subsidize employers, so that they take on new employees, than to aid the young jobless. Nevertheless, budget appropriations for this purpose have not produced spectacular results because of the huge disproportion between the number of young unemployed and the very small number of new jobs created. Another reason is the resistance of employers, who are always anxious to keep their wage bill to a minimum. Thus in the United Kingdom, whereas there were about 600,000 schoolleavers in 1975, employment subsidies granted over a period of six months to the private sector resulted in the recruitment of only 30,000 people.

Continued vocational training ('recurrent' education)

Continued vocational training is a necessity in itself, regardless of the employment crisis. It allows workers to adapt to new technologies, to improve their knowledge or to retrain. But in a period of unemployment the outlook for 'recurrent' education or continued training is very different: there is absolutely no certainty of finding or returning to a job after a course of training. These courses really allow only a 'rotation' of the jobless, for whom they constitute merely an individual and short-lived palliative. [1] But while recurrent education disguises some of the unemployment, it does not stimulate the creation of jobs, and cannot therefore be considered as helping to resolve the employment crisis. This 'rotation' of the jobless is illustrated by the measures adopted by the Swedish Government to have young unemployed people hired in the place of employees who are taking training courses.

The same is true in France, where subsidies and various benefits are granted to those who employ young people under a 'job-training contract'. These are not highly educated young people, and nothing guarantees that they will keep the jobs once the benefits cease. Lastly, the number of trainees is too small to be able to say that the system has attained its objectives.

Non-traditional occupations

This type of activity is on the increase. It includes small, part-time occupations (child-minding, various services), work connected with handicrafts and cultural activities (leather working, dressmaking, drama) or public-spirited activities which are not strictly necessary (restoring districts or villages, social work in towns, helping the aged, family planning, etc.). Some of this work receives government aid. In Canada, public-spirited work by young people is encouraged and partially paid; steps to support handicrafts have been taken in France. This kind of work is attractive to young people because it gives them opportunities for creative activity, or a chance to feel socially useful. Tasks are not fragmented; they do not consume time in the same way, and the individual is not weighed down by authority.

On the other hand, the common factor in all this non-traditional work is that it is underpaid, or not paid at all. The young people's interest in the work leads them to a self-

1. It is obvious that the majority of people out of work have no possibility of taking training courses or returning to school.

exploitation which cannot last for long. This recourse to voluntary work not only relieves public services and the State from the obligation to give financial support, but it is also more or less bound to fail during a time of crisis affecting employment and workers' purchasing power.

Thus these parallel occupations, in spite of their attraction for the young, cannot last long or develop further, for they are based on underpayment of work potential which is unacceptable to young people and workers generally.

Job creation in the public sector

Proposals of this nature would provide a partial solution to youth unemployment, but they seem to remain erratic. No real steps seem to have been taken in this area; quite the reverse, public services and government departments tend to restrict their payroll and to limit considerably the employment of new staff. However, it must be stressed that such job creation would not be artificial, for the public sector is crying out for more staff and the service which it provides is deteriorating from one day to the next.[1] But government policy is geared to other objectives.

Social measures

Lowering the retirement age for all workers would allow a certain number of jobs to become vacant for young people; indeed, it is better for the community to support retired people than unemployed. And a reduction in the working week without a reduction in pay would have the same effect. But then one encounters the objections of employers, who mention their wage bill, and these measures are not adopted.[2]

1. In France, the experts preparing the Seventh Plan have estimated the most immediate needs of the health sector to be 120,000 new jobs and those of government departments to be 100,000 jobs (about 15 per cent of forecast unemployment figures). These prospects are not negligible, but it seems unlikely that they will be followed up.
2. The Emploi et Travail commission of the French seventh plan estimates that to lower the retirement age to 55 would free 200,000 jobs (the trade unions want retirement at age 60 for men and 55 for

The government action and proposals examined above amount to no more than transfers (of funds or of unemployed persons) and do not come to grips with the basic causes of the employment crisis. The subsidies and various benefits granted to the private sector to encourage it to create jobs (especially for young people) have so far had only very limited results. On the other hand, the help given to business companies for their restructuring is considerably greater, but it has not resulted in the creation of jobs. On the contrary, the concentration and winding up of businesses occasioned by restructuring results in staff cuts and dismissals.

Substitution of capital for labour

This effect is characterized by the growing amount of capital investment in plant, premises and raw materials in comparison with that put into remunerating work potential (wages and salaries). This accumulation of hardware does not necessarily increase a company's technical efficiency. A study devoted to French companies[1] points to a 'growth in productive investment which is more rapid than the real growth of the company, and on the other hand a decrease in the rate of activity which is parallel to the growth in the volume of gross fixed capital formation' (see Tables 11 and 12).

These two observations tend to confirm the theory that companies are engaged, in addition to making 'growth' investments, in making labour-saving 'productivity' investments. They are therefore at present directing their efforts towards favouring profitability over growth and, even within the framework of growth, towards pursuing profitability as an objective. They thus need to make a maximum reduction in their staff and their wage bill. Hence the remark by Marc Bormann:

women), and that a reduction of the working week to forty hours, offset by increased productivity, would allow the creation of 180,000 job vacancies. These two measures would absorb more than 20 per cent of the unemployed.

1. J. C. Vassal, 'La Stagflation, une Analyse de l'Expérience Française, 1964-1974', *Problèmes Économiques* (Paris), No. 1457, 28 January 1976.

56   *Simone Morio*

The capitalist method of implementing technological progress and increasing productivity is maximum accumulation of the means of production (dead labour) with a corresponding elimination of living labour—that is, workers to operate the means of production; and the maximum exploitation of this living labour so as to extract the highest gain from it.[1]

This phenomenon of accumulation of goods and capital is the basic cause of unemployment and of the deterioration in the working conditions of those who have a job. As Tables 11 and 12 show, the increase in productive investments bears little relation to the objectives of growth, but reflects the requirements of capital accumulation. Such a policy deprives the community of jobs and of the benefits of growth based on an increase in purchasing power. The basic cause of the recession is the contradiction which exists between the need for continuous growth and the reduction in the purchasing power and employment opportunities of the productive forces. This contradiction is the fruit of the unceasing efforts to accumulate capital. Seen in this light, the few government measures mentioned above are designed to give companies in the private sector the financial means to enable them to maintain their rate of accumulation, rather than to promote actual job creation or the up-grading of occupations.

A different employment policy

The renewal of economic growth, accompanied by job creation, particularly in the production sector, is an indispensable element in solving the problem of unemployment. This growth is all the more necessary because the needs to be met are already huge. Quantitatively speaking, the need for social, educational and cultural facilities, instead of shrinking during the crisis, tends to grow. Recreation, holidays and children's schooling increasingly become a luxury because of the erosion of families' purchasing power. Qualitatively, 'the very process of development implies a changing pattern of needs and con-

1. Marc Bormann, 'Crise, Chômage, Productivité' *Économie et Politique* (Paris), No. 266, September 1976, p.34.

Table 11. Substitution of capital for labour in France from 1964 to 1974

		1964	1965	1966	1967	1968	1969	1970	1971	1972	1973	1974
Changes in GDP volume	A	100	104.5	110.6	116.0	120.5	129.2	136.3	143.5	151.8	160.2	165.5
	B	—	+4.54	+5.75	+4.88	+3.93	+7.17	+5.50	+5.30	+5.81	+5.53	+3.28
Changes in the volume of productive investments	A	100	123.0	133.8	142.2	146.9	163.2	175.0	184.6	196.1	204.7	216.8
	B	—	+23.0	+8.90	+6.29	+3.28	+11.09	+7.25	+5.44	+6.23	+4.42	+5.90
Changes in rate of unemployment	A	100	123.6	127.4	164.5	192.6	150.5	156.8	194.2	212.3	192.1	211.8
	B	—	+23.58	+3.12	+29.08	+17.13	−21.87	+4.20	+23.84	+9.30	−9.52	+10.23

A = index of change, taking 1964 as the base year (100); B = percentage variation from one year to the next.

Source: J. C. Vassal, 'La Stagflation, une Analyse de l'Expérience Française, 1964-1974', *Problèmes Économiques* (Paris), No. 1457, 28 January 1976.

sumption';[1]   new types of consumption appear, which compensate for the deteriorating quality of life.

As has been stated, a slowing down of growth results in unemployment, and a growth which does not first try to satisfy domestic needs is bound to encounter insuperable obstacles. Exploitation and unemployment among workers are growing in all the industrialized capitalist countries, resulting in a drop in public consumption, aggravating the difficulties of finding outlets for production, and putting a powerful brake on growth. The fact that some firms are experiencing substantial growth means not that there is, or is going to be, a general resumption of growth but simply that these companies (and their countries) occupy a position of strength on the market with which they are concerned, i.e. the sharing of national and international markets has been in their favour. But these markets cannot develop further, and consequently the growth of the countries concerned cannot be pursued, if public consumption remains

Table 12. Acceleration in the substitution of capital for labour in France (annual rates of growth)

	1950-57	1957-64	1964-73
Growth of staff members	1.0	1.4	1.4
Growth of gross productive capital (constant prices)	3.4	5.3	7.0
Substitution of capital for labour	2.4	3.9	5.5
		1961-67	1967-72
Productivity of labour		4.7 per cent	5.7 per cent

Source: Comité Emploi et Travail, *Emploi et Travail—Préparation du VIIe Plan*, Table No. 13, p. 42, Paris, La Documentation Française, 1976, 410 p.

1. Commission Emploi et Travail, *Emploi et Travail—Preparation du VIIe Plan*, p. 165, Paris, La Documentation Française, 1976, 400 p.

curbed by unemployment and the down-grading and exploitation of work potential. The recommendations in the working paper submitted to the EEC Labour Conference (June 1976), stipulating that 'Europeans must work harder and save more, invest more and consume less', are therefore doomed to failure if their objective is to solve the problem of employment.

Growth based on the satisfaction of needs is not only necessary, it is possible. It should be noted, in the first place, that the working population is increasing. According to the experts in the EEC Commission on Labour Prospects (October 1976), there will be an average rate of increase of from 0.6 per cent to 0.7 per cent a year for the period 1975–80; the total number of jobs must therefore rise by about 7 or 8 per cent by 1980—an increase of 1.5 per cent a year. The proportion of graduates within this working population will also increase: 'Between 4 and 10 per cent of the young people entering the European labour market are university graduates.'[1]

On the basis of these facts, 'what makes sustained growth necessary, makes it possible; . . . . the needs to be met, a young working population which is growing and which has received a longer training, and production arrangements which are being modernized',[2] all these factors permit continuous growth. On the other hand, to make use of only a fraction of the work potential of a country increases the social cost of non-workers to be borne by the workers, whereas this ratio would tend to decrease in certain countries as a result of the full employment of the working population (see Table 13). The situation could no doubt only improve if a more favourable policy were pursued with regard to the employment of women, which would allow the right balance to be maintained between workers and non-workers, even if the retirement age were to be lowered, since the numerical increase in retired non-workers would be largely offset by women, who form a substantial reserve labour force, taking up employment.

There are thus needs to be met and hidden productive forces to permit substantial and sustained growth. The point at

1. See 'Chômeurs, ce n'est qu'un Début', *Economia* (Paris), No. 28, November 1976.
2. Commission Emploi et Travail, op. cit., p. 166.

Table 13. Number of non-workers per 100 workers in some OECD countries

Country	1965	1970	1975	1980	1985 (projections)
France	137.6	136.9	137.1	135.6	133.7
Federal Republic of Germany	116.2	129.2	134.8	134.2	133.0
Italy	150.2	162.2	177.8	178.2	177.2
United Kingdom	109.3	117.9	122.0	121.0	119.3
Japan	103.5	95.2	99.9	106.7	111.6
United States	152.1	141.2	134.5	130.7	132.6

Source: OECD, *Evolution Démographique de 1970 à 1985 dans Quelques Pays de l'OCDE,* Paris, 1974.

issue, and the stumbling block to such growth, is the nature of production relationships. To seek immediate, maximum profits leads, as has been seen, to the restructuring of capital and the abandonment of certain sectors of production in order to strengthen others which are in a better position internationally, to the substitution of capital for labour—whence fewer jobs, down-grading of jobs, exploitation of workers and finally, wastage of the human and physical resources of a country.

A different employment policy is feasible only if the aim is the better and greater satisfaction of the people's needs and if economic growth is based on investments affecting employment, improved working conditions, education and vocational training. It is by using and developing the abilities of individuals, instead of limiting the number of graduates and down-grading work potential, that a society can grow and satisfy its own as well as external needs. In this sense, the struggles of workers who are anxious to preserve the value of their work potential, the number of jobs and the level of vocational training, have a positive effect on economic trends. They succeed in maintaining or intensifying the use of human abilities in employment; this has repercussions at the level of needs and consumption and gives new impetus to various markets.

To sum up, a different employment policy implies the

quantitative and qualitative development of the use of men's working abilities:

By raising the general standard of learning of all individuals.

By developing vocational training on this basis of general learning.

By analysing the conditions which have allowed the compartmentalization and down-grading of jobs, so as to achieve a new distribution of tasks and new working methods.

By giving priority to the development of employment in manufacturing industry, while not neglecting the exploitation of national resources (agriculture, energy sources, etc.), by making full use of existing means of production and by capital investment, with a view to creating jobs in these sectors, possibly with State aid.

By creating jobs in the public services (health, teaching, research, tele-communications, etc.) and in social, cultural and leisure activities.

By re-opening domestic markets through a social policy on wages and employment.

Within this framework, more specific measures concerning young people could be taken; but they will not bear fruit unless the environment is one in which priority is given to growth and the development of production forces. One could mention particularly the following measures:

A minimum income could be guaranteed for young job-hunters.

The government could recruit large numbers of young people in occupations for which it has responsibility.

In the private sector, employers could be required to engage young people in permanent jobs.

An improvement should also be made in working conditions (pace of work, safety precautions), in the content of work and in labour relations (redefinition of posts, information for workers about day to day management, and discussions about decisions concerning their company, redefinition of management roles).

Jobs for young people should not be subject to any discriminations as regards level of pay, nature of responsibilities, promotion prospects.

Specific training courses for young people should be instituted and paid for by the State and employers.

Contacts should be established between universities and
employers, with a view to making it easier for young people
to find work, so long as guarantees are given that the
universities will preserve their autonomy in relation to the
employers in question.

All these measures should promote economic recovery and a
decrease in unemployment, particularly among educated young
people. However, they would not further return on the ideal of
maximum capital invested.

Conclusion

In conclusion, the author would like to sum up the ideas expressed earlier in this study.

The level of education is not a sufficient factor to protect a young person from unemployment, learning no longer fulfils its function of social advancement. Degrees are depreciating on the labour market, not basically because of their subject matter, but because the structure of the labour market places workers in competition with one another, and this is even more true as the labour market contracts. Rather than the inability of education to adapt to working life, it is the inability of the economic system to provide sufficient jobs to satisfy the demand which results in unemployment (especially among young people) and the devaluation of degrees.

While inequality—due to the course of study followed, to social background, etc.—characterizes the employment situation of young people, the basic causes of unemployment are the same for everyone: the young are the last to arrive on a saturated labour market which is incapable of absorbing new labour because of economic recession, and which is putting a brake on productivity in order to maintain the short-term profits of top industrial and financial groups at the international level.

The work refusal found among some young people is not, contrary to what one sometimes reads,[1] the fruit of changing

1. 'Many individuals lack the faculties necessary for them to take their place in the economy, both because of the greater degree of specialization required and because of changing ideas and customs. This personal inadequacy aggravates the consequences of a certain lack of adaptability of secondary preparation for entry into working life.'('Le Marché du Travail aux Etats-Unis', *Revue Économique de la Banque Nationale de Paris* (Paris), January 1974.)

customs which destroy in them the faculties they need in order to enter the world of work. In the circumstances, this is not a question of personal inadequacy. This refusal is rather a social and economic phenomenon, occasioned by the discrepancy which exists between, on the one hand, the aspirations of young people as far as jobs are concerned and, on the other, the tasks and working conditions which are offered them. Because of the general raising of the educational level, today they both want, and are capable of doing, work which requires greater knowledge, is more varied, less monotonous, and provides scope for creativity and personal initiative; the jobs they are offered, however, are often less and less skilled, and are to be performed in unpleasant working conditions.

The introduction of new technology increases the number of unskilled jobs. This is not inevitable. Seeking maximum profits, employers reduce salary costs and, with this aim, adopt techniques and methods of work which, through a growing compartmentalization of tasks, devalue work potential. They could think up different 'job profiles', but that would entail higher salary costs and would necessitate longer and more expensive vocational training.

Education is not at present oriented in this direction. It encourages ever earlier diversification and specialization, which clearly reflect the economic objectives and the increasingly marked division of labour found at all levels. But this excessive specialization, which is not based on a sufficiently broad multi-disciplinary theory, constitutes a handicap for workers faced with the introduction of new techniques or the need to retrain. Only an education which avoids premature compartmen-talization, which is directed towards the scientific disciplines and provides everyone with a multi-disciplinary grounding, would allow speedy adaptation and mobility of workers, young ones in particular.

If there is 'overproduction' of degrees at the moment, it is in relation to the short-term needs created by an economic policy concerned with maximum return on capital. But this policy is marred by internal contradictions. Graduate unem-ployment, like measures to reduce the number of degrees awarded, can only shackle scientific and technological develop-ment. Since the various countries are at different stages of development, technological backwardness prejudicial to industrial activity may obtain in any sector. This policy aggravates the discrepancy between the needs of an expanding society and the possibility of satisfying them; some experts even predict a future shortage of technicians if such a policy were to be pursued.

The labour market is today saturated in almost all socio-professional categories and in numerous branches of activity. The fact that the recession is almost universal proves that the crisis in the developed market-economy countries is profound and long-lasting. The production apparatus is the first to be affected by this recession. The closing down of mines and factories is becoming more frequent in these countries; but the recession also affects the movement of capital (banking, trade, etc.). In other words, the crisis is not restricted to one branch of activity, it is not isolated. All the links in the capital chain—the manufacture and movement of goods—are affected: the whole system is unhealthy. The moderate recovery which can be detected is taking place without creating any jobs or any really new industries. It is geared to the growth of productivity and making work potential profitable.

Governments are investing considerable amounts (some-times in the form of job-creation subsidies) to help the leading sectors which are competitive internationally. However, this effort is being made at the expense of other sectors (that of energy, in particular). This high cost of the imports which have become necessary may oblige governments to revise this policy and re-invest in these neglected areas. On the whole, these contradictions, which are inherent in the search for short-term profits, cause a substantial waste of resources. Economic recovery of this sort cannot last, for it is not based on a recovery in public consumption, which is a determining factor of growth. Focused essentially on the growth of high-yield investments, it speeds up the trend of substituting capital for labour and of making global work potential profitable.

Governments contribute to this trend by imposing austerity measures on the workers. They block pay rises without taking parallel steps to subdue inflation; they raise direct and indirect taxes; they decrease 'social payments' and reduce social facilities and services. All these factors plunge domestic markets into stagnation, and make an extensive and lasting production boom difficult, if not impossible. If there is a recovery, it is an artificial one, since it is based on inflation and the speculation which is encouraged by international monetary instability.

Growth also helps to fan the flames of inflation by the very mechanism of investment. This is because the immobilization of ever greater amounts as fixed capital gradually reduces variable capital, which is the only creator of wealth. The desire to maximize immediate profits leads to an accumulation of capital goods which can take place only with increasing State aid—hence the phenomenon of inflation. Contrary to what some people say, it is therefore not the increase in total wages which is 'the principal cause of the continual rise in costs and prices',[1] but the growth of investment in fixed capital (plant and premises) and the accumulation of such capital.

This contradicts the theory of the need for a 'new social contract' to conquer inflation and the social perils which go with it (unemployment, decline in purchasing power). In the United Kingdom, for example, the social contracts concluded between the trade unions and employers in no case halted inflation or the rise in unemployment. A new social contract based on 'a new and fairer distribution of income'[2] would result, above all, in a redistribution of exploitation among the various categories of worker. This has been the case, for example, in the Federal Republic of Germany where, although the spread of wages is narrower than in France, young employees still suffer from real discrimination, while unemployment also continues to be rife in the country, especially among young people.

Some politicians recommend that, in order to end unemployment, employment should be treated as a 'strategic variable and no longer a dependant factor, an objective and no longer an instrument of economic adjustment'.[3] It seems impossible to reach such an objective by voluntary means. This

1. T. Balogh, 'Inflation and the New Economy' *Challenge—Magazine of Economic Affairs* (London), November-December. 1973.
2. Ibid.
3. P. Mauroy, 'Pour une Politique de l'Emploi', *Le Monde* (Paris), 25 June 1976.

objective echoes the recommendations made to governments,[1] aimed at achieving an internal restructuring of jobs in a company and an improvement of working conditions. Such hopes are praiseworthy in themselves but cannot be realized except in an isolated and temporary fashion, unless at the same time steps are taken to encourage public consumption and revive economic growth, primarily in the manufacturing sector and on the basis of national resources.

The same is true for the argument based on the 'policy of the best job'. To solve the problem of employment, this policy must be part of a policy of growth, lower unemployment and recovery of consumption. Any attempt to adopt one of these political options independently of the others seems doomed to failure.

1. See in particular, Commission Emploi et Travail, op. cit. Part 4.

Select bibliography

Bastide H.; Roset-Cazenave M. *Formation et Devenir Professionnel d'une promotion de Jeunes après des Études Courtes.* Paris, Institut national d'études démographiques, La Documentation Française, September 1972.

Berman, Kavn. *Structural Unemployment in the United States.* Washington, D.C., Department of Commerce, U.S. Government Printing Office, 1976. 122 p.

Boccara P. *Études sur le Capitalisme Monopoliste d'Etat, sa Crise et son Issue.* Paris, Editions Sociales, 1973. 450 p.

Brimer, M. A.; Pauli L. *La Déperdition Scolaire: un Problème Mondial.* Paris, Unesco/IBE, 1971.

Centre d'Études et de Recherches sur les Qualifications. *Accès à la Vie Professionnelle: Enseignement Technologique Long du Second Cycle.* Paris, La Documentation Française, January 1973. 160 p.

——— *Les Possibilités d'Emploi Selon les Qualifications Acquises dans les Formations Initiales.* Paris, La Documentation Française, June 1972. 147 p.

——— *Accès à la Vie Professionnelle.* Paris, La Documentation Française, January 1973, 160 p. (Dossier No. 5.)

Comité du Travail Féminin. *Le travail des Femmes en France et dans le Monde.* Paris, La Documentation Française Illustrée, No. 278, April 1973, 95 p.

Couetoux M. *L'Analyse des Emplois et des Formations de Niveau Supérieur.* Paris, Bibliothèque du Centre d'Études et de Recherches sur les Qualifications, Vol. No. 6, 1973. 110 p.

Gordon D. M. *Theories of Poverty and Underemployment. Orthodox, Radical and Dual Labor Market Perspectives.* Lexington, D.C., Heath, 1972. 177 p.

Gordon, Margaret S. *Higher Education and the Labor Market.* New York, 1974. 630 p.

Hugues P.; Pent G. *Les Emplois Industriels: Nature, Formation, Recrutement.* Presses Universitaires de France, Paris, 1973. 515 p.

Jeunesse Ouvrière Catholique. *Étude sur les Conditions de Travail de la Jeunesse Ouvrière en France.* Paris, Ministère du Travail, de l'Emploi et de la Population, 1973. 226 p.

Lantier F. *Le Travail et la Formation des Femmes en Europe.* Paris, Bibliothèque du Centre d'Études et de Recherches sur les Qualifications, Vol. No. 4, 1972. 67 p.

Michen F. *Chômeurs et Chômage.* Paris, Presses Universitaires de France, 1975. 290 p.

Piore M. J. *Notes for a Theory of Labor Market Stratification.* Massachusetts Institute of Technology, 1973, 40 p. (Working paper No 110.)

Pohl R.; Thelot C.; Jousset S. *L'Enquête Formation-Qualification Professionnelle de 1970.* Paris, Institut National de la Statistique et des Études Économiques, 1974.

Princeton University. *Scholarship for Society: A Report on Emerging Roles and Responsibilities of Graduate Education in America.* New York, 1973.

Rousselet; Balazc; Mathey. *Les Jeunes et l'Emploi.* Paris, Presses Universitaires de France, 1975. 410 p. (Cahiers du Centre d'Études de l'Emploi.)

Sullerot E. *L'Emploi des Femmes et ses Problèmes dans les Etats Membres de la Communauté.* Paris, 1973. 50 p.

Thomas, Jean. *Les Grands Problèmes de l'Éducation dans le Monde. Essai d'Analyse et de Synthèse.* Paris, Unesco, Presses Universitaires de France, 1975.

Valle-Kawecki. *Le Chômage aux Etats-Unis.* Paris, Presses Universitaires de France, Paris, 1972. 96 p.

Wood John. *How much unemployment? The Methods and Measures Dissected.* London, Institute of Economic Affairs, 1972.

ARTICLES

Balogh, T. Le Dilemme Plein Emploi-Inflation en Grande-Bretagne. *Problèmes Économiques.* (Paris), No. 1373, 22 May 1974, p. 27-31, (Previously published in *Challenge, The Magazine of Economic Affairs.)*

Debaisieux H. Le Chômage en Irlande. *Problèmes Politiques et Sociaux* (Paris) No. 121, 14 April 1972, p. 24-25.

Echo de la Bourse. La Montée du Chômage aux Etats-Unis, *Problèmes Économiques* (Paris), No. 1409, 12 February 1975, p. 11-13.

Flower, J. Le Chômage des Jeunes dans la Communauté Européene. *Lettre de l'OCIPE KASET DIENST.* (Strasbourg), No. 51, 24 November 1975, p. 109-14.

Frankfurter Allgemeine Zeitung. Le Chômage des Ingénieurs, Techniciens, et Jeunes Diplômés aux Etats-Unis. *Problèmes Économiques* (Paris), No. 1264, 22 March 1972, p. 28-31.

Hamm, W. Les Responsabilités de l'Etat dans l'Apparition du Chômage Structurel en RFA. *Problèmes Économiques.* (Paris), No. 1440, 1 October 1975, p. 20-3.

Kolm S. C. La Théorie de la Courbe Inflation-Chômage. *Revue Économique* (Paris), Vol. 21, No. 2, March 1970, p. 295-309.

Lefournier. L'Économie Française Pourra-t-elle Fournir du Travail à tous ceux qui en Demandent? *Problèmes Économiques.* (Paris), No. 1425, 4 June 1975, p. 6-12.

Mincer, J. Determining the Number of 'Hidden' Unemployed. *Monthly Labor Review* (New York), Vol. 93, No. 3, March 1973, p. 27-30.

Pellegrin; Praderie. Quels Services la Planification de l'Éducation peut-elle Rendre pour Améliorer les Relations entre l'Éducation et l'Emploi? *Lettre de l'OCIPE KASEF DIENST.* Strasbourg, No. 51 24 November 1975, p. 115-23.

Perspectives Économiques de l'OCDE, Population Active et Chômage dans le Pays de l'OCDE, *Problèmes Économiques* (Paris), No. 1457, 28 January 1976, p. 30-2.

Quelques Coûts Sociaux du Deuxième Miracle Allemand. *Problèmes Économiques* (Paris), No. 1440, 1 October 1975, p. 15-18.

Reich, M.; Gordon, D. M. ; Edwards, R. C. Dual Labor Markets. A theory of Labor Market Segmentation. *American Economic Review* (New York), Vol. 63, No. 2, May 1973, p. 359-65.

Revue Économique de la Banque Nationale de Paris. Le Marché du Travail et la Politique de l'Emploi aux Etats-Unis. *Problémes Économiques* (Paris), No. 1362, 6 March 1974, p. 12-21.

Salais; Eymard-Duvernay. Les Relations Complexes entre les Creations d'Emplois et l'Évolution du Chômage en France. *Problèmes Économiques* (Paris), No. 1419, 23 April 1975, p. 14-19.

Vassal, J. C. La Stagflation, une Analyse de l'Expérience Française (1964-1974). *Problèmes Économiques* (Paris), No. 1457, 28 January 1976, p. 2-8.

Volz, J. La Crise Économique Italienne. *Problèmes Économiques* (Paris), No. 1398, 27 November 1974, p. 19-23.

Unemployment among educated young people in the French-speaking developing countries

Yarisse Zoctizoum

Introduction

Inflation and unemployment are two plagues which have for several years afflicted the so-called 'market-economy' countries, whether they be 'developed' or 'undeveloped'. Hence the outcry and questions from all sides: Are we moving towards an economic slump like the one of 1929? Will history repeat itself? Is petroleum responsible for the present situation, or could it be the incompetence of rulers, the selfishness of employers, the demands of trade unions, the deterioration of the terms of trade? Should we blame the content of education, which is ill-adapted to employment? Are there many countries which are unable to catch up with capitalist technology? These are some of the questions, being asked today by the development specialists and authorities in the market-economy countries, observing that the unemployed today number more than 30 million in these countries.

Unemployment, which has been on the increase for several years in nearly all the market-economy countries—developed and undeveloped—seems to have dampened the enthusiasm long displayed by the proponents of economic growth. It has become a primary concern in these States, to the point where all of them, during the World Conference on Employment organized by the International Labour Office in June 1976, recognized implicitly the failures of the development strategies adopted and advocated until now—especially in regard to 'developing' countries. Instead of bringing prosperity to workers, these strategies did nothing but mask reality:

Conscious that development strategies in the past have not led to a diminution of poverty and unemployment in most of the developing countries; that in those countries, the historic methods of development have given rise to an employment structure characterized particularly by a strong concentration of labour in rural areas, with high levels of under-employment and unemployment; that underemployment and poverty in rural areas and in the non-structured urban sector, and the avowed unemployment, particularly in urban zones, have attained such critical dimensions that major changes in the strategies of development on the national and international scale have become urgent in order to assure as rapidly as possible the full employment and a sufficient income for every inhabitant of our planet.[1]

The conference also stated that it was 'conscious that industrialized countries have not been able to maintain full employment and that economic recession has engendered wide-spread unemployment.'[2]

After this admission of failure, a 'more equitable inter-national economic order' is now being contemplated. Is this the beginning of a new mystification of the workers, or the end of an injustice that can no longer be concealed? Rampant unemployment is accompanied by a rise in prices of all products—even staple products which were formerly available to the most underprivileged masses. And at the same time we are witnessing the collapse of numerous theories which were previously advanced by the 'market-economy' economists and doctrinarians on the subject of unemployment and its remedies. This situation is complicated by the development of unemployment among young people: first, young workers and farm labourers, without education, who often understandably rebel, and, recently educated young people and young graduates who are disillusioned with the myth 'an academic degree means employ-ment'.

It is in this context that the author was asked to study unemployment among young people in relation to the content of education, principally in the French-speaking developing countries. There must, however, be in the offices of national and international organizations and ministries concerned many recipes for solving the problem of employment for young

1. ILO, *World Conference on Employment*, *Geneva, June 4-17, 1976: Summary Report No. 20.*
2. ibid.

people, but they are doubtless destined to suffer the same fate as the strategies whose failure was mentioned at the International Labour Organization (ILO) conference. No attempt will be made therefore to devise another solution or to produce statistics on the unemployment of the young; indeed, this would be impossible, for only one Unesco Member State from the area considered responded to the inquiries made by the organization.

The present analysis of the unemployment of educated young people will therefore deal mainly with the significance of the development of unemployment among the young, throughout the world and particularly in the French-speaking developing countries. Special attention will be devoted to its objectives causes—economic, social, political and ideological. This study will deliberately leave aside all subjective considerations such as the opinion which the jobless may have about their status or the arguments which employers may put forward in order to justify their own behaviour in particular instances. Only an investigation covering society as a whole, the economic system, the method of production and the social relationships of production, can clarify unemployment and its significance; no formulas based on speculation and abstract reasoning can help us to understand this phenomenon, still less to solve it. Through these 'causes' we shall see the dual 'function'—national and international—fulfilled by unemployment in the market economy countries which form part of the French-speaking Third World.

General remarks

ARE THE GENERAL PROBLEMS OF YOUNG PEOPLE ISOLATED PROBLEMS?

At the beginning of the nineteenth century, it was common for children to be employed in industry, often from the age of 6. In addition, there was no retirement: working life was practically the entire life of the individual. But it should be noted that the use of children of that age did not have as its primary aim the enrichment of European societies in general, or the broadening of the child's mind. It was aimed above all at profit, the expansion of capitalism and 'liberation' with respect to pre-capitalist family relationships. Certain factories of that era, notably in England, preferred therefore to hire children and women, who were 'docile' workers and were always paid less. It was thus easy to break strikes of adult workers and force them into prolonged unemployment. But as a result, on the one hand, of the development of productive forces, better organized struggles by workers and the crash of 1929, and, on the other hand, of the 'democratization' of education, children and young people in general found themselves gradually withdrawn from industry. Compulsory military service also contributed to this result. Thus the myth of youth and its own problems was born.

First of all, the need to teach all citizens how to read, write and count and to give them a minimum basic knowledge led to the 'democratization' of education and lengthening of the period of study which precedes the commencement of working life. Next, attention was devoted to the young people who had just left school and could not find work. For example, since the 1950s, capitalism, endeavouring to restructure the labour market, transforming work conditions in general and constantly seeking new openings, invented a 'youth market' which it inundates with consumer goods destined for young people: magazines, television and radio programmes, records, and multiple gadgets, clothes, cosmetics, etc., all disseminating and instilling a conception of the world peculiar to young people. These two phenomena—lengthy schooling cut off from production (a real 'training centre' for the jobless) and ideological conditioning of young people through advertisements of all kinds—led certain specialists to describe young people as a 'new class', which should be offered a 'common cultural model', implying the right of young people to be different from or even possibly 'against' adults. From that time on, the problems of youth—but what youth?—have been presented as isolated problems, in no way linked to the nature of society. Thus characterizing young people in the abstract, the experts are quite incapable of finding adequate answers to the problems of these young people, which are in the last analysis problems of society. Young people are not all cast in the same mould. Indeed, is not the first difficulty to define the age bracket that comprises young people? Each country, quite legitimately, wants to define it in terms of its own particular circumstances. After all, what is true for youth is true also for all other social categories, strata or classes: they can be dealt with only in the context of society as a whole.

In all market-economy countries, unemployment among young people is today a distressing problem. To be sure, some self-righteous people still claim that 'if the young are unemployed, it is because they have difficulty adapting to new situations and they no longer want to work as their worthy parents did'. But such an explanation is incompatible with the figures in Table 1.

Furthermore, in absolute figures, the number of young jobless today far exceeds in all countries the number of adult jobless while, according to the same source, the 15-25 age group accounts for only between 20 and 35 per cent of the working-age population. In addition, the countries which have a high percentage of unemployment increase (as shown in Table 1) are countries where unemployment appeared only recently but developed at an amazing rate.

Table 1. Percentage increase in unemployment from 1973 to 1974

	Young people (%)	Total (all age groups) (%)
Belgium	64	33
Denmark	405	261
France	77	57
Federal Republic of Germany	210	154
Italy	12	5
Ireland	121	31
Luxembourg	69	102
Netherlands	61	40
United Kingdom	13	2
Average	49	32

Source: Commission of the European Communities, supplement to document V/456/75, p. 1, Brussels, 6 May 1975.

In the Third World countries—from non-socialist Asia to Africa and Latin America—the situation is more serious: some 50 to 80 per cent of young people are unemployed, which is double or more than double the number of adults unemployed. Finally it should be noted that in these countries the population is on average very young. The myth that young people are a new class conceals many realities: youth in the slums, immigrant youth, rural youth, young people driven from their ancestral land, young people whose country is ravaged by a war waged in the name of so-called 'modern values', young people whose only fault is that they are different from others, etc.

Therefore it is in the very structures of the various societies—all over the world—in which these young people live that we must seek the causes of the unemployment afflicting them and it is at this level that the problem must be solved.

SOME CHARACTERISTICS OF THE ECONOMIES OF 'DEVELOPING' COUNTRIES

It cannot be emphasized too often that nearly all the countries which have for some years been called 'underdeveloped countries', 'developing countries', 'poor countries', 'the Third World', etc., share a long historical experience. They were conquered and subjected to the colonial yoke, to the extermination and deportation of a large part of their population, more or less complete destruction of their way of life, forced insertion into a capitalist-world economy and, finally, restructuring of their economy to meet the demands of the great powers. This historical evolution admittedly led to political independence—for example, in the French-speaking countries of Africa. But their economy is still generally characterized by underdevelopment and therefore by a state of dependence on the industrialized countries.

In these French-speaking countries, growth is based primarily on external demand—that is, on exports of their raw materials (peanuts, cocoa, cotton, coffee, copper, iron, uranium, timber, etc.) and on foreign financing or, in other words, on imports of capital. This input of foreign capital is facilitated by investment codes which ensure the rapid recovery of costs and the repatriation of all profits. Without forgetting other forms of dependence (cultural, ideological, technological, military, etc.), two forms will be stressed in particular: commercial dependence and financial dependence. The first is reflected in a transfer of assets to the profit of the industrialized countries, for the former colonizing powers and the multinational companies keep raw material prices very low and benefit from the enormous differences in the remuneration of work, with equal productivity, which exist between the poor countries and the industrialized countries. This transfer also takes place through worker emigration, which is draining the developing countries.

The financial dependence of these countries is total. O. Lebrun notes that, in the nine French-speaking countries of West Africa, between 1960 and 1970 more than 70 per cent of investments was financed from abroad, while the local ruling classes were placing their capital in foreign banks. In addition to these 'procurement costs' there are operational subsidies

from abroad to stabilize public finances.[1] How could these
countries not be in a permanent external payments crisis? With
a few rare exceptions, they suffer from a current trade deficit.
Imports always tend to increase more rapidly than exports; in
addition, repatriated profits are generally greater than the
inflow of foreign capital: for the whole of French-speaking
West Africa, during the last decade, repatriated profits
increased by 3.8 per cent a year but the inflow of foreign
capital increased by only 3.2 per cent.

The French-speaking countries of Central Africa are particularly affected by this situation. The trade deficit is always
accompanied by a deficit in public finances. Current expenses
to run the State machinery are enormous, out of all proportion
to the material base of the economy, which in any case is geared
to a foreign market. The economy is generally depicted as a
'dualist economy', composed of a 'traditional' sector and a
'modern' sector; or as a 'disjointed economy', characterized on
the one hand by the existence of millions of small farmers with
rudimentary tools, organized to some extent in village communities, and on the other hand by a national and/or foreign
sector which is much better equipped. Theoretically, small-scale
handicrafts, small or large national industries (private or public),
semi-public corporations, foreign companies, large multinational
units, etc., exist side by side. In fact, one can no longer speak
of 'traditional' or 'dualist' economies in Africa, for each small
farmer or craftsman is linked today by the monetary economy
to the world capitalist system. There is thus no reason to
compare the 'traditional' and 'modern' sector. The 'disjointedness' of sectors and economic units is the inevitable result of
these countries' integration in the international capitalist
division of labour. Their economy cannot be different from
what it is unless there is a dialectical break with the world
capitalist market, involving an internal change in production
relationships.

This 'disjointedness' of the economy of each country

1. O. Lebrun, 'Les Stratégies de Développement Extraverti', *Une Autre
    Education pour la Jeunesse: Formation-Action pour le Développe-
    ment*, Dakar, Unesco Regional Office for Education in Africa (Round
    Table organized from 7 to 12 February 1972.)

prevents the formation of national markets and even of an inter-African market. Thus, in 1974, according to the World Bank, only 4.6 per cent of exports from all the African countries went to other African countries (scarcely $1,600 million compared with about $35,000 million to non-African countries).[1] The easy repatriation of capital therefore leads to the specialization of economic activities, in a competitive international market organized for the benefit of the multinational corporations and especially of the former colonizing powers. Examples are plentiful: phosphate in Morocco, iron in Mauritania, copper in Zaire, petroeum, timber and uranium in Gabon, coffee and cocoa in the Ivory Coast, etc.

Socially, specialization and domination are in general reflected in a very uneven distribution of productivity and income as between the different sectors and the different social strata. In Africa, the agricultural sector contributes less than 40 per cent to the national product in most countries, whereas it usually occupies 90 per cent of the so-called working population: consequently, agricultural productivity is very low. At the same time, the social transformation of the rural world is accompanied by a high rate of unemployment badly controlled, because it stems from the constraints imposed by the external market. Prices of agricultural products have been at a standstill since 1950, while the cost of imports has continually increased. The low salaries imposed during the colonial era have not changed since then. The result is ever-growing poverty among the masses and offensive wealth among the essentially administrative and military 'bourgeoisie' responsible for maintaining political and social order. Barely 7 per cent of the inhabitants of these countries hoard more than 40 per cent of the income. Thus the masses feel, at the grass roots level, the effect of the slightest national or international economic crisis. Within the 'franc zone', for example, CFA francs (national currencies) depend on the French franc, just as the so-called central banks of those countries depend on the Banque de France.

To sum up, unemployment used to be unknown in this context (according to the settlers themselves, who often needed

1. Jacques Vigne, 'Le Commerce Entre Pays Africains', *Le Monde* (Paris), 10-11 October 1976, p. 17.

workers), but today it is developing very rapidly because of the
international economic crisis. It is in this light that one must
consider the problem of unemployment in general, and unemployment of young people in particular. But in these
countries, the majority of the population is young. It is therefore
difficult to distinguish between unemployment of the young
and unemployment of adults. This brings us back to the
question mentioned earlier: What category of the work force
does youth represent?

THE WORKING POPULATION AND UNEMPLOYMENT IN AFRICA

The African population

The African populations underwent terrible trials during the
colonial period as such, and continue to be bled by the new
forms of deportation consisting of internal migration towards
industrial centres and external emigration to industrialized
countries. In spite of high birth rate, Africa therefore remains
the least populated of the five continents, and the population
density is even lower in French-speaking Africa. This is undoubtedly already a factor of underdevelopment, contrary to
what demography experts believe. Nevertheless, it is comforting
to note that the birth rate remains high in all the African
countries, so that the age pyramid there has a very wide base.
For the whole of Africa, the African Regional Conference of
the International Labour Organization, held in Accra in 1969,
estimated the annual birth rate at 46 per mille (crude birth
rate—that is to say, the number of live births per thousand).
This rate is the highest in the world. Towards 1960, the rates by
country were between 35 and 59 per mille, even reaching 55
to 62 per mille for certain countries such as Nigeria, the Ivory
Coast, Togo, Mali and Zambia. On the other hand, the annual
death rate ranged from 14 per mille in Rwanda and Rhodesia,
to 35 per mille in the Ivory Coast and 40 per mille in Guinea.
Among thirty-eight countries surveyed, twenty-eight had a rate
of between 15 and 34 per mille, with an average of 23 per mille.
For the annual rate of increase of the African population, the
figures varied between 1.5 and 3.5 per cent in twenty-eight
countries (between 2.1 and 3.01 per cent in sixteen cases).

Table 2. Estimate of the net increase of the working population by sex for Africa as a whole and by subregion, 1960—80 (in thousands)

Subregions and Continent	1960-70			1970-80		
	Men	Women	Total	Men	Women	Total
West Africa	6,368	3,177	9,545	8,810	3,979	12,789
East Africa	4,130	1,550	5,680	5,212	1,872	7,084
Central Africa	1,107	428	1,535	1,436	531	1,967
North Africa	4,562	1,371	5,933	6,226	1,924	8,150
Southern Africa	1,165	366	1,531	1,513	489	2,000
Total	17,322	6,892	24,224	23,197	8,793	31,990

Source: ILO, *World and Regional Estimates and Projections of Labour Force,* 1966.

The estimates published by the United Nations[1] in 1966 forecast an increase of 2.6 per cent per annum for the decade 1970-80 and the highest rate in the world for the following decade. According to the estimates of the same organizations, the African population under 15 years of age will increase from about 155 million in 1970 to about 205 million in 1980. In these circumstances, it is not surprising that the majority of the unemployed today are young people.

Structure of the working population

According to ILO estimates, the working population of Africa, estimated at 112 million in 1960 and 136 million in 1970, will be in the neighbourhood of 168 million by 1980 (Table 2). The annual rate of increase of the total population is estimated at 2.4 per cent for 1960-70 and 2.6 per cent for 1970-80; that of the male working population is slightly lower (2.1 and 2.3 per cent respectively) and that of the female working population still lower (1.7 and 1.8). Therefore the male working

1. United Nations, *World Population Prospects as Assessed in 1963-64,* New York.

population, for the entire period under consideration (1960-80), must increase more in Africa than in the developing regions as a whole, although the rate of activity is to decrease from 41.1 per cent in 1960 to 39.4 per cent in 1970 and 37.5 per cent in 1980.

ILO also estimated that the 'rate of dependence' (total population for every 100 working persons) would increase from 243 in 1960 to 253 by 1970 and to 266 by 1980, mainly because of the growing number of young people under 15 years of age. Yet this last figure has already been far exceeded because demographic growth, urbanization, high youth unemployment, reduction in the number of junior officials (in certain countries) and rural underemployment due to low agricultural productivity often force many people to come and live near (and live off) a member of their family who is a wage-earner, especially in the urban areas.

It should be noted that the number of jobs created up to now is far from proportionate to the figures quoted above. In addition, the number of people abandoning working life is much lower (about half) than the number of young people entering the labour market. New jobs must therefore be created for half the young people. Since that has not yet been done, one can safely say that this proportion has now reached two-thirds. Taking into account population growth and job stagnation, out of 1,000 young people, 700 to 800 are not finding work—not counting those who are underemployed.

Unemployment of French-speaking educated young people and legal definitions of unemployment

THE CONCEPT OF UNEMPLOYMENT

Legal definitions

Since capitalism is developing at different rates in different places throughout the world, each country or group of countries tends to define unemployment in the light of its interests and its own circumstances. In Western Europe, the definitions are unambiguous; but in the Third World countries, they often go from one extreme to the other and the terms 'jobless' and 'unemployed' are sometimes set off against each other in order to prove that there are no unemployed! Consequently, a general definition of unemployment which confined itself to characterizing or describing its immediate causes and effects would be far from reflecting the realities of many countries; yet unemployment is indeed rampant in all market-economy countries, whatever their level. Nevertheless, the eighth ILO International Conference of Statisticians, held in Geneva in November-December 1954, did evolve such a general or 'universal' definition, which included various categories of unemployed. Not being able to reproduce the entire definition, we shall simply say, as did the French National Institute of Economic Studies, that the aforesaid categories include the following three conditions: to be fit for work and available, not to have a job, and to be seeking paid work.[1] In other words, an unemployed person is someone of working age, without employment and looking for paid work. It should be noted that the age limits (top and bottom) of working or professional life vary from country to country.

Moreover, several methods are used, according to the country, to count the number of unemployed. In France, for example, this is done either when they register on an administrative card-index (unemployed persons that might be termed 'in conformity with the regulations'), or when a population census is taken or surveys made on employment. The French-speaking countries have followed these methods, but they do not yield satisfactory results because the socio-economic structures in the countries in question are different from those in France; in addition, they do not have the necessary statistical infrastructure. It should be noted that, besides these legal definitions, the economists have worked out measuring instruments and concepts for evaluating and classifying different kinds of unemployment. They thus distinguish the following types: frictional unemployment (of very short duration, 'between jobs'), contingent or cyclical unemployment (due to a decline in activity, especially seasonal), structural or technological unemployment (caused by a change in conditions of production or by a restructuring of a business), concealed unemployment (underemployment that is not visible); marginal unemployment (as in the case of the spouse of a wage-earner taking up and leaving a job according to circumstances), and potential unemployment (married couples remaining at home, students who find no job and prolong their studies, 'somewhat excessively', etc.)

These are the legal definitions of the different categories of manpower, not being utilized or in reserve, used by the economists of the developed countries with a market economy. But these definitions are often applied in an arbitrary way to societies at an intermediate stage which are very different from the societies for which the definitions were formulated. In

1. See Eloy Vandepotte, 'Ambiguités des Définitions du Chômage' *Sociologie du Travail* (Paris), July-September 1973, p. 293.

many countries of the Third World, and especially of Africa, the social and economic structure and the way in which they have been integrated in the world capitalist economy pose, on that account, a number of problems concerning the use of various concepts of foreign origin.

The concept of unemployment and the economic structure of the developing countries.

The concept of unemployment came into being with the capitalist mode of production—as did others, such as that of strike, for instance. It is therefore in terms of the accumulation of capital that it can be defined. Consequently, unemployment properly so called exists in fact in the developing countries, because capital there, both foreign and local, needs to increase and therefore to accumulate. But unemployment cannot be characterized there in the same way as it is in the market-economy countries. If, like them, we seek to define unemployment in 'behaviouristic' terms, that is to say, by emergency, poverty, the pressing need for employment, etc., we are only touching on immediate causes. The developing countries cannot and must not do this, not only for the reasons already mentioned, but also because any definition of the kind formulated by the Geneva conference overlooks a large part of the real problem in their case, since in the French-speaking African countries only 5 to 10 per cent of the inhabitants are wage-earners. The others have no work and must either emigrate or else vegetate in the so-called 'traditional' or handicrafts economy. As regards underemployment, if the same meaning were attached to this concept in French-speaking Africa as in Europe, it would be found that only 4 to 5 per cent of wage-earners (who represent a mere 10 per cent of the population) are actually working, which is not the case. But the notion of working hours, the conditions of work and the exploitation of workers are such in these countries that capital derives considerable profits from them (otherwise, it would invest elsewhere). Hence, 'underemployment', far from being an effect of underdevelopment, is a condition of the development of capitalist relations.

Unemployment, in these countries, is due to the internationalization of capital, i.e. investments of foreign origin and the transfer of profits to foreign countries. Unemployment is not, let us repeat, 'an effect of underdevelopment'. Some economists claim that it is, and then assert that the said unemployment and the 'technological backwardness' explain 'underdevelopment'—a sophism which is also a vicious circle. In reality, unemployment performs a precise function in capitalist development: it is at the same time the condition for the start of a cycle of development and the outcome of that same cycle. In the countries under consideration, it serves to keep permanently in reserve an army of potential workers, subject to various forms of exactions and forced labour within the country, or transferable abroad, more especially to the industrialized countries of Europe.

The work of young people in the pre-capitalist economies of Africa

Before describing the character of unemployment among young people today, it is desirable, on the one hand, to define the concept of work and place it in its context and, on the other, to recall briefly what the work of young people in Africa meant before the introduction of the capitalist mode of production or 'market economy'. A tiresome tendency to generalize this notion of work is to be noted among the experts on development; but actual work, its physical expression, does not have the same meaning in all modes of production, nor from one country to another and, still less, for all social classes. In some regions of the world, manpower consisted chiefly of slaves, considered as mere means of production in the same way as the horse, the ox, the ass. In the feudal countries of Europe and elsewhere, work was the lot of the serfs and was called 'servile work'. In both cases, this term was synonymous with constraint and suffering for the one class (slaves and serfs), because they were working for masters; for the ruling classes (masters and feudal lords) to work with their hands meant losing caste.

At the beginning of the capitalist era in Europe, Judeo-Christian morality, basing itself on the Biblical curse condemning man to earn his bread in the sweat of his brow, presented work to the 'new slaves' as a sacred means of 'redeeming original sin'. As to the philosophers and politicans of the eighteenth and nineteenth centuries, they made of it a virtue, based on an individual or social morality. Later on, work was extolled as the best way to get rich, and today, in all the market-economy countries, it is chiefly seen as the way to individual success ('work means social advancement'), while in countries with a planned economy, individual labour tends to become a means of collective success. It is thus clear that the content of the notion of work varies according to the period and the economic regime. On the other hand, it should be pointed out that work understood in the absolute sense of the term, that is to say, the labour force as such, deprived of means of action and not directed to a particular object—a production target—does not suffice to secure social advancement, whether individual or collective. A combination of certain conditions is necessary if work is to bring some advantage to the worker himself and to his community. These conditions are of an ideological, political, economic and social kind. In short, both work and unemployment are linked with the nature of society.

In traditional African societies, apart from some countries where house-slavery and feudal systems were the prevailing regimes, work had a social character which many specialists in African history and ethnology have not failed to note. And in our time, African social formats, at least those that have not been completely destroyed by the capitalist system, still bear witness to that fact. In Africa, as a general rule, the basis of socio-economic organization was the village community, and the principal unit of production was the family or the community itself. Consequently, from his childhood, the youngster was associated with production in the context of the technical and social division of work. First, it was from his parents and his elders that he learnt to farm, to hunt, to fish, to cut wood, to make war, to distinguish right from wrong. Education was closely related to production and, apart from the stories told in the evening—which moreover had a close connection with social activities—was acquired in the very place where the work was done. In this regard, A. Moumouni writes: 'The efficacy of this education was rendered possible only by its intimate relationship with life. It was through social acts (production) and social relations that the child or adolescent was always educated'.[1] In these conditions, work was not a process of private appropriation of nature, of wealth, or of another's work, but a process of social integration. The young, the aged, adults—all had to work, each at his own level, and it was through this kind of collaboration that each village community felt that it existed with respect to others. No one 'went into retirement', school was not cut off from production, working life merged practically with the whole existence of the individual. The notion of work was therefore extremely different from that which obtained in the countries which practised slavery and in feudal, then capitalist, Europe.

It was not, of course, perfect bliss; and we are not recalling the past with nostalgia. But it is impossible to understand the sudden rise in unemployment among young people without taking a look at the past. In the period of direct colonization, children were always associated with the work of the adults, and there were very few modern schools—barely enough to meet the needs of the settlers. The index of activity of young people of both sexes was higher in agricultural countries—usually colonized countries—than in industrialized countries—usually capitalist countries—as Table 3 shows.

But, today, the indices of activity shown in Table 3 no longer correspond to the facts. Young people—and especially young educated people—are more and more swelling the ranks of the unemployed.

Underemployment or the industrial reserve force in French-speaking Africa.

Before the Second World War, and still quite recently, the problems of unemployment and of underemployment, and the possibilities of creating new openings and paid jobs, interested no one in Africa, especially in French-speaking Africa. Apart from forced labour for everyone, emphasis was placed on the persistent lack of manpower with which colonial governments and private enterprises had to cope. There was therefore no talk of underemployment or of unemployment and still less of

1. A. Moumouni, *L'Éducation en Afrique*, p. 34, Paris, Maspero, 1964

Table 3. Indices of activity by sex and by age about 1952

Age Group	Industrialized countries		Agricultural countries	
	Men	Women	Men	Women
10-14	4.1	2.4	23.9	10.2
15-19	12.4	53.6	78.4	30.9
20-24	91.5	51.9	91.2	31.5
25-34	96.7	30.3	96.3	29.9
35-44	97.6	28.3	97.5	30.6
45-54	95.9	28.1	96.3	28.9
55-64	85.6	20.8	91.6	23.7
65 plus	37.7	7.1	70.1	14.3

Source: Bowen-Finegan, *The Economics of Labor Force Participation*, Princeton, 1969.

'economically active population'. The rare 'development' plans which came to light made no attempt to take account of the manpower factor because the practice of forced labour made it possible to have as much unpaid manpower as was necessary, and the fate of workers mattered little.

On the other hand, working conditions and working time did not correspond to the wishes of the colonists. Climatic conditions, vegetation cycles, the means available to the peasants, their way of life and their system of values determined their working time, which therefore varied from one region to another. In such a context, the concepts of unemployment and underemployment, of economically active or non-active population were meaningless. In reality, there was no lack of manpower because it could be had under constraint. The situation has changed in the last few decades. The populations have gone from one tragedy to another—from forced labour to lack of work—and there has been no improvement in this respect with the accession to political independence. Thus the concepts of underemployment (visible or concealed), of unemployment, of 'economically active' population, etc., have made their appearance in Africa, at a time when forced labour, having ceased to play its chief role—namely, the destruction or deformation of the precapitalist socio-economic structure—has changed its aspect and when, commercial and capitalist relations having sufficiently developed, villagers and towndwellers alike have become dependent on local capital and especially on foreign capital.

Henceforth, therefore, it is in terms of capital that we must speak of underemployment and unemployment. However, the concept of underemployment does not fully explain the fact that most workers depend on capital even if some of them own their land, their small means of production. Underemployment is only a material instance of the process by which capital sets up a reserve of manpower, on a national and international scale. According to the economists, underemployment is chiefly located, in Africa, in the rural areas where technical progress has hardly made its way and where productivity is low. But in the towns, it also affects those people who earn their living from 'marginal' occupations and 'small trades': shoeblacks, street vendors of cigarettes and newspapers, pedlars, car washers, bicycle, sewing machine or refrigerator repairmen, small craftsmen (tailors, jewellers, coach-builders, electricians, blacksmiths, cabinet makers, mechanics, etc.). This is the so-called 'non structured' urban sector, apparently away from the main stream of economic growth and on the fringe of industry. Workers in this sector are rarely included in the lists drawn up by statisticians and thus escape taxation. But if, in fact, the statistical infrastructure is still inadequate in these countries, whose fault is it? The 'invisible hand' of capital has already found its way there, and it is through the intermediary of these 'small trades' that, led by this invisible hand, commercial and capitalist relations have penetrated to the grass roots. It is certain, however, that this sector does not fall outside the scope of the 'law of growth' of the economists, since given the economic level of these countries, it plays the part of sub contractor. Moreover, the workers belonging to this sector are subject to taxation and to all the hazards inherent in the practices of the national and international market. Lastly, ILO experts have noted that this sector obtains from 24 to 30 per cent of the total jobs in the cities of Kenya, more than 30 per cent in Abidjan, 25 per cent in Calcutta (in 1969), more than 40 per cent in Jakarta, etc.

Far from falling outside the scope of the 'law of growth', the situation of these workers merely illustrates the contradiction of growth. It is therefore difficult to describe this situation as one of underemployment and low productivity. Here we must go back to the term 'reserve force', with its able recruiters: yesterday forced labour, today school. More and more, in towns and in rural areas, young people are becoming educated but finding no employment. They therefore emigrate: in Africa itself towards the large centres, then to Europe. In any case, the capitalist accumulation necessarily produces throughout the world an 'overpopulation' which forms an inexhaustible reservoir of available manpower, one that is docile and transferable from one country to another. This overpopulation is in excess only in relation to the national and international needs of capital, and not—as attempts are often made to lead us to believe—in absolute figures, or because it would exceed the possibilities of the production of means of subsistence. Public authorities today recognize that underemployment, hitherto attributed to archaic or traditional methods of production, is engendered by capital. This is confirmed by the systems of assistance, grants and allowances, both public and private, which are allocated to the unemployed in all the developed capitalist countries.

As regards the remedy, this is surely not to be found in the struggle against underemployment in itself, or in birth control. As an old African proverb says: 'The more numerous the helping hands, the bigger and fuller the granary'.

THE DEVELOPMENT OF EDUCATION AND EMPLOYMENT IN THE FRENCH-SPEAKING COUNTRIES OF AFRICA

Development of education

As everyone knows, the capitalist type of education was unknown in Africa before the arrival of the colonists; it was they who introduced it, chiefly for the training of their servants: guards, clerks, interpreters, business employees, etc. Very soon, the economic needs of the colonists gave rise to a considerable expansion of this education. None the less, Africa remains the continent with the lowest rate of school enrolment.

Lè Thành Khôi notes in 1963, that the rate of enrolment was less than 9 per cent of the total population, as against 13 per cent in Asia, 16 per cent in South America, 18 per cent in Europe, 21 per cent in the Soviet Union, 22 per cent in Oceania, 26 per cent in North America; and that higher education, in the same year, represented only 0.9 per cent of the total population, as against 1.9 per cent in South America, 2.2 per cent in Asia, 3.5 per cent in Europe, 4.4 per cent in Oceania, 7 per cent in the Soviet Union and 8.6 per cent in North America.[1] At that time, Africa had around 306 million inhabitants. Little was said about unemployment, although it already existed.

Accession to independence, the ever more rapid development of the commercial and capitalist economy, the lack of trained personnel, and the people's desire to learn, gave a new impetus to education—an impetus that was in fact relative, since in 1970, the young people not attending school still represented more than 62 per cent of the population in the age groups corresponding to primary education. For thirty-five African countries, that amounted to some 23 million young people.

In 1972, André Lemay, of the Unesco Regional Office in Dakar, gave for Africa south of the Sahara the following rates of school enrolment: 8-21 per cent, seven countries; 24-33 per cent, eleven countries; 49-71 per cent, fourteen countries; 87-93 per cent, only three countries. The author concluded: 'Despite all the efforts made in favour of education, primary schooling is now finding, in most countries of the region, its expansion curtailed, slowed down and sometimes blocked.'[2] In regard to secondary education, its advancement has been much more rapid, in the French-speaking countries, than that of primary education; but, as Lè Thành Khôi notes again, this very high rate of advancement is due to the fact that the number of pupils at secondary level was very low to begin with

1. Lè Thành Khôi, *L'Enseignement en Afrique Tropicale*, p. 21, Paris, Presses Universitaires de France, 1971.
2. André Lemay, *Formation-action pour le Développement*, p. 19, Dakar, Unesco Regional Office for Education in Africa, February 1972.

in many countries (in 1950, for example, 146 pupils in Mauritania and 106 in Chad: 50 pupils more give a growth rate of 35 per cent and 50 per cent respectively). On the other hand, in absolute figures, the number of pupils is still minute by comparison with the mass of children of school age. Today these rates are dropping. As a rule, they do not reflect the actual situation as regards schooling. In 1961, the Conference of African Ministers of Education meeting in Addis Ababa fixed, as objectives, raising the rate of primary school enrolment from about 40 to 71 per cent by 1970, with the aim of approaching 100 per cent by 1980. Simultaneously, secondary-school enrolment was to be stepped up to about 15 per cent by 1970. But the Round Table on Training and Development—convened by Unesco in 1972 in Dakar—was to point out, to the great surprise of the ministers of education, that in Africa south of the Sahara, in 1970, the rate of primary-school enrolment had only reached 49 per cent instead of 71 per cent, and that of secondary-school enrolment 7 per cent instead of 15 per cent, whereas the number of children not attending school was, as we have said, 23 million. There are still, therefore, enormous efforts to be made, at both the secondary and the primary levels, and still more if it is recalled that the adults, for the most part, are also illiterate. Lastly, in higher education, the advance has undoubtedly been greater than at the primary and secondary levels, but the number of students is still very low. Moreover, the universities and other establishments of higher education—which have become more numerous in the French-speaking countries of Africa since their accession to independence—are very costly for the national budgets and are still far from being able to remedy the shortage of competent senior staff, which accounts for the prolonged presence of numbers of foreign executives in these countries.

Technical education, at the primary, secondary and higher levels, is progressing with difficulty, is still adapting itself poorly to the economic structure of these countries and lagging behind general education. P. Hugon[1] noting this lag in a

---

1. P. Hugon, 'Enseignement et Emploi à Madagascar à la Veille du IIᵉ Plan Quinquennal', *Revue Économique de Madagascar*, December 1971, p. 162.

country like Madagascar (though it also exists in all French-speaking countries) writes:

The lag between general education and technical education can be assessed by comparing some significant figures. In 1969, of the 19,217 candidates for the middle-school certificate (BEPC) 470 were from technical education. There were only 1,493 candidates for the middle-level vocational qualification (CAP). In the same year, only 22 candidates sat for a technical secondary-school leaving certificate and 2,258 for the secondary-school leaving certificate in general education. Among university students, 25 per cent are studying science as against 75 per cent studying liberal arts, law and economy. Thus technical education accounts for less than a seventh of the total number.

This form of development, characterized by imbalance between the different levels, preference accorded to general education, dropping out at all levels and the existence of 'prestige' universities and centres of higher learning, is very costly for the African States. The education system absorbs more than 25 per cent, and sometimes 30 per cent, of their budgets; of course it provides jobs for a large number of workers, but it in no way stimulates development. In addition, it imposes a heavy burden on poor families, since the shortage of premises, teachers and equipment, on the one hand, and the strong social demand, on the other, have caused numerous private schools to spring up, which are very profitable for their owners. P. Hugon notes that, in Madagascar,

children from poor homes pay school fees of about 15,000 Malagasy francs a year, while their family's income is between 10,000 and 20,000 Malagasy francs a month. This leads to the paradoxical situation that the paying school is often supported by the less well-off. The turnover of private undenominational education was estimated at 1.2 billion Malagasy francs in 1966, representing a profit of 450 million. [1]

The rising cost of education, which is observable everywhere in Africa, is due chiefly to the increasing number of private technical-education institutions. The trend of educational development is therefore far from corresponding to the evolution of the labour market. It has its own logic, as does the

1. Hugon, op. cit., p. 164.

labour market. Thus we see growing up a new category of jobless, namely that of young people who are educated.

The structure of employment and the labour market for young people

In 1960, the so-called economically active population was distributed as follows: 71-86 per cent in agriculture and 6-10 per cent in industry. This applies to all the African countries except the Republic of South Africa. In the same period, in Europe, 14 per cent of the workers were engaged in agriculture and 39-45 per cent in industry. The regional conference of the ILO, mentioned earlier, noted that in East Africa, the percentage of wage-earners was lowest in Ethiopia, Madagascar and Uganda. In West Africa, the Ivory Coast, Ghana and Liberia were the countries where paid employment was the most developed: about 13 per cent in the case of the first and about 20 per cent in that of the other two. Nigeria, more densely populated, had in absolute figures more than a million wage-earners, but the structure of employment was the same there as in the other countries. In Central Africa, about half of the wage-earning active population was concentrated in Zaire, the most densely populated country of this subregion. Wage-earners (all branches of activity) represented about 20 per cent in Zaire and Gabon, of which some 15 per cent worked in non-agricultural branches. In roughly half of the thirty-four countries studied, the proportion of wage-earners was less than 9 per cent of the active population, and the proportion of non-agricultural wage-earners less than 7 per cent. Some exceptions were, however, noted. Apart from the Republic of South Africa, two countries had a high proportion of wage-earners: Mauritius, where 85 per cent of the active population were in paid jobs (of which 50 per cent were in the non-agricultural sector), and Egypt, where 50 per cent of the active population were wage-earners (30 per cent in the non-agricultural sector).

Generally speaking, the structure of the active population in the developing countries is marked by the predominance of paid employment in the sector of services (trade, transport, public and private services) at the expense of the industrial sector (factories, manufacturing industries, building, transport,

Table 4. Evolution of employment in Africa, 1960-80 (in millions of persons and in percentages)

Regions	Sectors	1960		1970		1960-70[3]		1980		1970-80[3]	
		M[1]	%[2]	M	%	M	%	M	%	M	%
West Africa	Primary	25.9	70	29.7	65	3.8	41	35.2	60	5.5	41
	Secondary	3.8	11	6.0	13	2.2	24	9.2	15	3.2	24
	Tertiary	7.1	19	10.3	22	3.2	35	14.8	25	4.5	35
	Total	36.8	100	46.0	100	9.2	100	59.2	100	13.2	100
Central Africa	Primary	8.8	70	9.7	66	0.9	45	10.7	63	1.0	40
	Secondary	1.3	10	1.8	12	0.5	25	2.4	14	0.6	24
	Tertiary	2.5	20	3.1	22	0.6	30	4.0	23	0.9	36
	Total	12.6	100	14.6	100	2.0	100	17.1	100	2.5	100
East Africa	Primary	19.6	71	21.8	67	2.2	47	23.9	62	2.1	32
	Secondary	2.8	10	3.7	12	0.9	19	5.7	15	2.0	31
	Tertiary	5.2	19	6.8	21	1.6	34	9.2	23	2.4	37
	Total	27.6	100	32.3	100	4.7	100	38.8	100	6.5	100
North Africa	Primary	13.3	63	15.8	58	2.3	41	18.1	52	2.8	34
	Secondary	2.6	13	3.9	15	1.3	23	6.1	17	2.2	26
	Tertiary	5.1	24	7.1	27	2.0	36	10.4	31	3.3	40
	Total	21.0	100	26.8	100	5.6	100	34.6	100	8.3	100
Total	Primary	67.3	69	76.5	64	9.2	43	87.9	59	11.4	37
	Secondary	10.5	11	15.4	13	4.9	23	23.4	15	8.0	26
	Tertiary	19.9	20	27.3	23	7.4	34	38.4	26	11.1	37
	Total	97.7	100	119.2	100	21.5	100	149.7	100	30.5	100

1. M: million persons (underemployed included).
2. %: proportion of persons employed in relation to total employment.
3. Number of additional jobs, by millions, during the decade.

etc.). The regional conference of the ILO noted that the manufacturing industry occupied the first or second place among the providers of non-agricultural paid jobs in eleven countries; building occupied the second place in ten countries, and trade in two countries. In Morocco, the transport sector held first place by providing 40 per cent of the total non-agricultural paid jobs. According to the estimates of the development experts, the evolution of employment between 1970 and 1980 should be much the same in all the large regions of Africa. If the present tendency continues, agriculture will still account in 1980 for a very large part of the total employment—60 per cent on average. By that same time, the tertiary sector will occupy about a quarter of the employed population, and the secondary sector will be content with the remainder, approximately 15 per cent. On the other hand, agriculture will absorb a little less than 40 per cent of the total number of additional jobs, and the tertiary sector 40 per cent: a high level of urban underemployment will thus come into being, since the secondary sector will absorb only about 25 per cent of the additional jobs, as shown in Table 4.

If Table 4 is compared with Table 2, a large difference can be seen between the increase in the active population—about 24 million from 1960 to 1970—and the number of additional jobs created during the same period—21.5 million. For the period 1970-80, the corresponding estimates are about 32 million and 30.5 million respectively. At the end of the 1960-70 decade, the figures recorded by the demographers even exceeded the estimates in regard to the increase in the active population, while the rate of wage-earning activity decreased in several countries. If account is also taken of underemployment and a standstill in employment (the index of activity would have moved from 41.1 per cent in 1960 to 39.4 per cent in 1970), it may be said that today more than half if not two-thirds of the active population is not working. As the active population is generally very young in these countries, the proportion of unemployed young people may be estimated at 70 per cent, of which 80 per cent are among the 'educated young people'. It should be noted that the official figures are far from reflecting the real situation, given the conditions in which the survey was carried out and the number of undeclared unemployed. The situation is therefore becoming more and more serious in French-speaking Africa, where industries were already rare in the colonial period. Consequently, the poverty of the masses increases every day, and the numerous development projects have been unable to check this trend.

Such is the context in which the labour market for educated young people is set. In rural areas, the young people cannot hope to find work, since the economic activities are still chiefly food-crop farming, cattle raising, fishing, handicrafts and small trades. The few new jobs created in rural areas (in education, administration, plantations, co-operatives, etc.) are far from being able to absorb all the educated young people from the rural environment—who, moreover, think they can do better in town—they therefore emigrate in large numbers to the towns, as do the other young people. Forced labour and the depopulation of the African countryside have prevented agriculture from developing in a way calculated to produce jobs. On the contrary, its scant progress and the quasi-stagnation of prices imposed on the peasants have merely driven the latter to the towns. Hence, the urban population in Africa has increased rapidly, although this continent is still little urbanized (2 per cent of the total population in 1930, 9 per cent in 1960 and 15 per cent in 1970). In urban areas, the creation of jobs depends chiefly on national and international investments. In the public sector, the evolution of employment is related to the budget level and to external aid. Although a number of posts became available, after the accession to independence, by reason of the Africanization of staff, this situation has now come to an end and no longer offers openings. In some countries officials are even being dismissed in sectors such as telecommunications and certain civil service departments.

Qualifications, salaries of young people and the 'brain drain'

The lack of competent staff and skilled workers, often referred to in Africa, has been one of the factors which have speeded up the development of education on this continent—as, indeed, in all the Third World countries. Since the accession to political independence, the problems of development have clearly been

Table 5. Degree of qualification of African manpower in 1965
(in percentages)

	Unskilled workers	Skilled workers	Technicians	Staff and senior staff
Central African Republic	67.0	26.0	2.5	4.5
Eastern Cameroon	69.7	24.6	2.1	1.8
Western Cameroon	67.6	22.3	9.9	1.9
Ivory Coast	60.0	20.3		19.5
Benin	70.0	10.0	1.3	2.0
Gabon	69.1	23.9	1.6	2.0
Mali	72.9	24.9	1.7	0.5

Source. Lè Thành Khôí, *L'Enseignement en Afrique Tropicale*, p. 316,
Paris, Presses Universitaires de France, 1971.

related to this condition: economic 'take-off' necessitates the
training of large numbers of staff and especially of skilled
workers. It is undeniable that this problem still exists today
after some years of independence. Table 5 gives a general idea
of the number of skilled workers in some countries in Africa
a few years ago.

It will be seen that 14 years ago, 60 to 70 per cent of wage-
earners were unskilled. Despite the development of education,
the number of skilled workers is still quite insufficient because
factories, which are increasing in number in Africa, are intro-
ducing new techniques. This highly important problem of
training has been treated case by case and not as related to all
sectors of the economy. Once more the easy way out has been
chosen, and training has been identified with education or
general education. The result is that many young people leave
school—even the few technical schools that exist—without being
able to find a job because their knowledge remains abstract and
bookish. To make up for this deficiency, it is thus still necessary
to call on foreign workers (mostly Europeans) who are often
of mediocre ability. While development calls, in all sectors of
the economy, for skilled workers, middle-level personnel and
business managers, more and more young people finishing their

primary and secondary studies do not succeed in finding a job. To solve this problem, all that is done is to set up so-called 'vocational training' centres, community villages, youth clubs, etc., which provide no more than a very theoretical training, since it is not related to the social and economic structure of the country concerned. On leaving these centres, young people often either find themselves idle or become office workers. Thus, without wishing it, they swell the number of administrative workers, while lacking the necessary qualifications and abilities. This brings to light the gaps in administrative supervision, the absence of a sense of organization, and the impossibility of giving administrative effect to decisions. It is in this way that corruption invades administrations.

Most States are affected by an acute shortage of university graduates and skilled manpower, especially in technical occupations. Paradoxically, the 'brain drain' is increasing. For political or financial reasons, African graduates prefer to stay in the foreign country where they have done their higher studies. African technicians, engineers and doctors are therefore numerous in Europe. This trend is explained by individual aspirations, but the main reason is political. It is the consequence of domination in their own countries by the foreign great powers. A survey carried out in France in 1968 revealed that 6.4 per cent of the total number of workers from Africa and Madagascar living in France consisted of persons belonging to the 'higher management' category. This proportion was nearly 60 per cent higher than that of French 'higher management' in relation to the active French population.[1]

In French-speaking Africa, the 'rationale' of the salaries imposed by colonization has been maintained, with the result that the difference between the highest and lowest salaries is enormous, ranging from 1,500 to more than a million CFA francs per month. Since the higher staff and the technicians are Europeans in the majority, most of the large salaries go to foreigners. Young graduates, in whom no ideal has been inculcated, aspire to the same occupations and the same salaries, which is understandable, even when they do not have the

1. *La Migration vers la France des Cadres dans les Professions Scientifiques et Médicales*, Paris, IRFED, 1968.

required qualification. (This explains their refusal of certain occupations and therefore, in part, unemployment.) In regard to university graduates, their migration is accounted for, in some cases, by essentially political motives but, in most cases, by the fact that they are paid less than their European colleagues having the same diplomas as themselves and working side by side with them. In this respect, it may be wondered whether co-operation does not bring with it the seeds of unemployment and of the migration of talent.

In Africa, salaries have not been adjusted for years past. The income of peasants who harvest agricultural products for export is also at a standstill, because the prices of these products have remained stable, if they have not actually lowered. The real purchasing power of rural people consequently diminished by 30 per cent from 1961 to 1967 (by 50 per cent from 1955 to 1967); today it must be still lower. This explains two phenomena: the stoppage of production of agricultural products for export, and a falling back to the so-called subsistence economy. The level of wages and of selling prices for agricultural products hardly encourages young secondary-school leavers to return to work in country districts or to accept certain types of occupation. On the other hand, the job market is very limited and the ideal that these young people may cherish in regard to the building up of their country fades when they see how the dominant social classes and the privileged live.

Are young people throughout the world in the same situation with regard to employment?

Basically, it may be said that the working class and the proletariat in general are in the same situation with regard to employment, because they have nothing to sell but their labour. But, as a consequence of their separation according to sex, age, even race, economic sector, trade, technical level—in short, the social division of capitalist labour—these different groups do not experience the same difficulties in this respect. Thus, women, young people, skilled workers, emigrants, country dwellers, etc., may find themselves in an ambiguous situation in the present circumstances. On the one hand, they are very vulnerable to unemployment because they can easily be laid off; on the other hand, at a time of crisis, they can be used to break strikes, check pay rises, and force those who are in employment to work more.

Young people are likewise divided. First of all by age groups, of course, but also and especially according to social origin, diplomas, qualifications, economic sectors and regions. It may also be said of young people that they are not all in the same situation with regard to employment. In Africa, as everywhere, the sons of government ministers and of higher officials are absolutely safe from unemployment; young people holding a university degree are less vulnerable—the percentages prove it— than those holding secondary or primary-school leaving certificates; the most seriously affected are young people with diplomas or certificates who come from poor families (petty farmers, workers, minor officials). When the ethnic or racial factor comes into play, the situation becomes grave. This factor plays an important part in French-speaking Africa in the distribution of employment.

Unemployment among educated young people

ASSESSMENT OF UNEMPLOYMENT AMONG YOUNG PEOPLE HOLDING DIPLOMAS OR CERTIFICATES

Any attempt to assess unemployment in Africa, and particularly in the French-speaking countries, comes up against two main kinds of difficulty: (a) the absence or inadequacy of statistics, which characterizes African economy; (b) problems of a theoretical kind which we have already tried to define and to which we shall not return.

In Africa, as a general rule, statistics relating to unemployment are mainly furnished by employment agencies, which are sometimes in an early stage of development; in the present state of affairs, these statistics only partially reflect the real situation. Moreover, workers are little inclined to use the services of these agencies, for several reasons: absence of relation between registration with them and the system of unemployment insurance (when one exists), absence of a public system of insurance, considerable qualitative imbalance between supply and demand in the labour market, and fear of being registered solely for the needs of the Treasury (for even the jobless without resources have to pay taxes). They therefore prefer to look for work on their own. Lastly, the employment agencies are usually of recent creation and are only to be found in the larger towns.

In regard to surveys, they are difficult to carry out. Investigators are always unwelcome to the local authorities, who fear that their questions may 'put ideas into the heads' of the people interviewed. It is therefore not surprising that only one country answered the questionnaire sent out by Unesco for the purposes of the present study on unemployment among young people in its Member States.

Here various factors of a socio-economic nature, always misapprehended by the local authorities, also come into play. The first is usually the heterogeneity of the unemployed population, where, side by side with a worker possessing a recognized qualification (however small it may be) and who has lost his job, we find the rural immigrant who does seasonal or permanent work, the boy under 14 years of age who cannot continue his studies, the former school-boy who is scarcely literate, another who has completed his primary studies, the student who has been through several years of secondary schooling and who would accept any job but finds none, another who refuses to do manual labour or who is waiting for his 'chance', etc.

The second factor consists in the relations of solidarity, still relatively important in some regions, which play the part of a system of unemployment insurance, sparing the local authorites certain expenses and social difficulties. But this solidarity is on the wane as a result of the development of commercial and capitalist relations.

The third factor is the important role of the so-called 'non-structured' sector (that of small trades) considered by economists as the 'refuge' for those who hope to find a better job later in the modern sector. This sector, where people are 'underemployed', contains the reserve manpower on which the capitalist sector draws.

For all these reasons it is difficult to establish exactly the number of unemployed, whether in country or in town. Nevertheless, some techniques such as sample surveys give an idea of the tendency and magnitude of the phenomenon. Young people with diplomas, or simply educated, whom these countries 'turn out' without having regard to their real needs, seem to be the chief victims. Generally speaking, the rate of unemployment among educated young people is between 50 and 80 per cent, taking underemployment into account. The following are some examples:

People's Republic of Benin. Among people seeking employment (women included) under 25 years of age, officially registered in the city of Cotonou alone, in 1975, 80 per cent had the school-leaving certificate or its equivalent, 18 per cent a certificate of secondary studies and 2 per cent a diploma of higher studies. In the same city, out of 5,740 requests for jobs registered from January to September 1975, 3,074 were from people under 25 years of age (2,574 young men and 500 young women).

Morocco. According to the governmental plan for 1968-72, 142,000 young Moroccans would reach the working age each year, for only 97,000 new jobs; hence 45,000 more jobless young people every year. But these figures are far from indicating the whole situation: underemployment in this country would seem to exceed 50 per cent.

Tunisia. The rate of underemployment in agriculture is 66 per cent.

Algeria. The rate of underemployment in agriculture is 69 per cent, and where the total number of unemployed has been estimated at between 1.5 and 2 million, the majority of whom are educated young people. It is therefore not surprising that so many young North Africans emigrate to Europe and especially to France.

Ivory Coast. Louis Roussel notes[1] that, despite the prosperity attributed to this country, in 1970 the city of Abidjan alone had 50,000 unemployed of whom only 10,000 were adults having lost their jobs; the 40,000 others (80 per cent) were young people between the ages of 15 and 25 seeking their first job. Abidjan must have today more than 90,000 unemployed.

Upper-Volta. Ambroise Sougré notes[2] that the number of young people reaching the working age represent from 3 to 4 per cent of the total population, or not less than 150,000 to 200,000 individuals each year, whereas the possibilities of

. Louis Roussel, 'Employment Problems and Policies in Ivory Coast', *International Labour Review*, Vol. 101, No. 3, March 1970.
. Ambroise Sougré, 'Massive Emigration in Upper Volta—Facts and Effects', *International Labour Review*, Vol. 101, No. 3, March 1970.

finding employment are very slight. More than 80 per cent of these young people are therefore obliged to emigrate to the Ivory Coast, Benin, and France, etc.

Central African Republic. Out of more than 30,000 pupils who sit each year the competitive examination for entrance to the first year of secondary education, only 2,000 are accepted; the others cannot continue their studies and therefore swell the ranks of people seeking employment.

Madagascar. Because of the education explosion, the first primary cycle rejects each year 100,000 students on average, the second primary cycle 30,000, the first secondary cycle 10,000, and the second secondary cycle 2,000. Hugon estimates at 15,000 the number of jobs created each year in this country from 1970 to 1974, whereas the active population increases by 80,000 people per year and the urban population by 70,000; at the same time, 30,000 pupils leave school at the end of the second primary cycle and 10,000 at the end of the first secondary cycle. This author adds: 'It may thus be roughly estimated that one-sixth of the pupils holding the primary school-leaving certificate, and one-fifth of those holding the certificate of supplementary primary studies, will find paid employment in the coming five years; on the other hand, there may well be a shortage of technicians and of "higher staff".'[1]

Similar facts can be observed in the other French-speaking developing countries, as indeed throughout the Third World.

CHARACTERISTICS OF UNEMPLOYMENT AMONG YOUNG PEOPLE: COMPARISONS BETWEEN EDUCATED AND UNEDUCATED YOUNG PEOPLE

In Africa, as in the rest of the Third World, unemployment mainly affects young people—and more and more those who are educated. This is especially because the populations of these countries are in fact much younger than those of the Western countries (though in the latter also, more than 50 per cent o

1.   Hugon, op. cit., p. 186.

Table 6. Percentage of young people leaving rural areas, according to their level of education.

	Illiterate	Able to read and write	Holders of a school certificate
Boys	8	42	61
Girls	11	55	75

Source: Louis Roussel, 'Measuring Rural-urban Drift in Developing Countries', *International Labour Review,* Vol. 101, No. 3, March 1970.

the unemployed are young people). The education explosion and the 'diploma myth' have greatly helped to make this sector of the labour force highly mobile. Henceforth it is totally dependent on foreign or local capital and no longer confined to the so-called traditional economy. For a young person in these countries, unemployment is less to be feared when he has either had no education or a higher education. (In the latter case, he can resort to underemployment or to working abroad, and thus become part of the 'brain drain'). The risk of unemployment is the highest for a person who has had a medium education: enough to leave his village, but not enough (and without vocational training) to find employment in a town. Is the solution, then, to remain uneducated or to pursue one's studies as far as possible? But how? Whatever may be the answer, the ignorant and scholars alike are prey to unemployment. The intensity of emigration, unemployment and underemployment thus seems to depend on the level of education, as is shown by Table 6 noted by Louis Roussel in the Ivory Coast.

This brings out the important part played by education as a factor in rural-urban drift. A similar phenomenon can be observed throughout the world. By way of example, Table 7 is taken from a study on unemployment in Sri Lanka.

According to Seers, at the time of the survey probably about one-third of university graduates were unemployed, the proportion being still higher among those with liberal arts degrees. And, during a mission to Colombia, he established the same facts as in Sri Lanka. In nearly all the countries of the Third World, therefore, a higher proportion of unemployment

Table 7. Open unemployment rates among young people by level of education reached, 1969-70 (in percentages)

Level of education	Age	
	15-19	20-24
None	23	8
Primary	34	15
Middle	46	39
Secondary (O-level)	92	63
Secondary (A-level)	—	27
All levels	41	34

Source: Dudley Seers, New Light on Structural Unemployment: Lessons of a Mission to Ceylon, *International Labour Review,* Vol. 105, No. 2, February 1972.

can be noted among persons who have a certain level of education. But these countries are becoming industrialized, and, at the same time, a growing number of new jobs can be noted as well as the hiring of foreigners in ever greater numbers. Thus, in Sri Lanka according to Dudley Seers, despite the presence of half a million unemployed properly so-called, the government of that country decided, in 1970, to recruit a great many Indian workers for various kinds of agricultural labour. Similarly in the Ivory Coast, in 1970, when there were 50,000 urban unemployed (of whom 80 per cent were educated young people), 70,000 foreigners were occupying posts in the town. There it was a question of very competent specialists (managerial staff, highly qualified persons, supervisors, technicians, etc.) needed by capital for purposes of management, and whom it was necessary to bring in from abroad. This phenomenon is curiously accompanied by an increasing growth rate in certain countries, which refutes the arguments of the proponents of economic growth about the growth rates that must be attained to make 'take-off' possible.

Girls have been hard hit by this unemloyment, despite the educational backwardness which is imposed on them in some countries. Educated girls are the first to be affected by unemployment and even by rural depopulation. They are often underemployed. Discrimination in respect of occupations and salaries affects them doubly: they are disadvantaged in relation to so-called 'qualified' foreigners, both men and women, and in relation to their fellow countrymen. As a rule, unemployment surveys are more concerned with young men than with young women. Women, in both urban or rural environments, form the bulk of the industrial labour reserve which capital sets aside for itself.

While unemployment among educated young people is evident, it conceals unemployment among the uneducated. The latter rarely register as unemployed, for fear lest the local administration may then, on their own authority, enrol them in the so-called 'vocational training' centres, 'village communities', 'young farmers' clubs', etc. In Black Africa there are more than 23 million young people from 10 to 25 years of age who have not attended school. Their situation is more serious than is generally thought. From the point of view of employment, there is little difference between them and educated young people. The reception centres—artificial creations—offer them nothing but a poor salary or free meals while they stay there. The training they are supposed to receive is theoretical, even if—in the village communities, for example—an effort is made to teach them to produce. When they leave, they are thrown back on themselves and find themselves incapable of setting up on their own account as craftsmen or farmers or of finding a job as a skilled worker. If some of them are taught a trade—to no purpose and with no relevance to any real socio-economic situation—this is aimed solely at making them mobile, at enabling them to change their place and status in the large reserve force to which they, like others, belong.

Lastly, something should be said about the relations between the trade unions and unemployed young people. Few are the unions that give their attention to, or have any concern for, unemployment among the young; usually, the leaders of these unions give their allegiance to the local authorities (government and employers), and are consequently unable to discuss on an equal footing with employers and the public authorities, or to wage real union campaigns against unemployment in general and unemployment among young people in particular. In the advanced capitalist countries, the trade unions seek to combat unemployment, and young people themselves are organized politically and have their own unions. They may receive compensation, unemployment benefits and public aid of various kinds. Of course, this assistance is not as a rule adequate as compared with the cost of living. But, in the developing countries in French-speaking Africa, such public aid, unemployment benefits, and the defence of unemployed young people—as well as the unemployed in general—by the unions, simply does not exist. The only source of help—which is moreover gradually disappearing—is family solidarity. The unemployed and their families are the ones who help the employers and the State.

The causes of unemployment among educated young people

The causes of unemployment have been implicitly apparent in all of the foregoing statements; we shall therefore sum them up in a few lines, since it is not possible within the limits of this work to undertake a detailed analysis. Attempting to explain unemployment solely by 'underdevelopment', and vice-versa, is simply going round in circles. As in all capitalist countries—advanced or not—there are two kinds of causes of unemployment: immediate or secondary causes and fundamental causes, inherent in the way chosen for development.

FUNDAMENTAL CAUSES

Is there any need to recall that the type of development chosen by the countries of the Third World or imposed by the former colonial powers is usually that of market economy? All the countries of the Third World which have opted for this way are experiencing, and will experience in one form or another, all the horrors that the developed countries have experienced in the course of their history and are still experiencing—with this difference that the former are in addition dominated, exploited by the great economic powers, at all levels and in all matters: commercial, financial, technical, military, cultural, political, etc. The structure of employment can only reflect this domination, at the level of the State, of private enterprises and of agriculture.

Unemployment—and in particular unemployment among young people—derives inevitably from this situation. Capital, in becoming internationalized, needs to create in all countries, and especially in the developing countries, a reserve force that is available for industry and that is both importable and exportable. Unemployment makes this availability possible. The disorganization (destruction/conservation) of the precapitalist economy, the 'dislocation' of the national economy by capital, the domination of industry over agriculture, the monopoly of technology and 'know-how', an incomplete education (i.e. one which merely reproduces the different classes and social strata instead of conducing to their elimination), exorbitant profits which are repatriated—such are the factors making for unemployment in these countries. It is thus impossible to speak of full employment there—which, moreover, no capitalist country has ever known. Unemployment will always result from the contradictions of capitalist economic growth.

IMMEDIATE CAUSES

In regard to immediate causes, it should be noted that monetary crises, the energy crisis, the petroleum price war, in short, the 'deterioration of the terms of trade', have very direct effects on employment in the Third World countries, because their currencies and the sale prices of their raw materials depend on the currencies and the decisions of the developed countries and the international trading companies. Unemployment and under-employment of young people in the agricultural sector and in certain public or private enterprises are caused by changes in agricultural prices and in prices of raw materials, and by the different forms assumed by the international economic crisis. But one of the most immediate causes of unemployment among young people in Africa is education.

As was mentioned earlier, the numbers enrolled in education at the primary, secondary and higher levels have increased relatively since the so-called developing countries have acceded to political independence. But, compared with the total number of young people of school age, they are still very low. This is the result of an education system the chief aim of which, in French-speaking Africa, was quickly to replace forced labour in its role as destroyer of traditional societies and creator of manpower for the colonists and the capitalist enterprises. Otherwise, how is it possible to explain the inability to provide work for so small a number of educated persons? Education in these countries was an element of the policy of colonization, so that its content, its organization, its relationship to employment (productive work) in no way served the interests of the workers, or even of those who were the first to be enrolled in school.

Once they had gained their political independence, these countries assigned themselves as a priority aim the generalization of education. They therefore maintained the organization and structure of colonial education, and in addition adopted, deliberately or under constraint, models of education appropriate to the advanced capitalist countries—with all their well known faults. As Lè Thành Khôi rightly notes:

The fundamental problem at present is that there is no African school or university; there is only a school or a university transplanted in Africa from abroad. But Africanizing education does not consist in replacing the *Le Roman de Renart* by *Les aventures de Leuk de Lièvre* (by Senghor), the names Pierre or John by Mamadou, wheat by millet, or even in increasing the time allotted to courses in African literature and history. Africanizing education means thinking it out in the light of the problems which these countries have to face and which require particular 'structures, programmes and methods'.[1]

It may be added that Africanizing also means changing the relations between classes and putting an end to economic dependence with respect to developed countries.

For several years past, it has been increasingly evident that selection is becoming established practice, that a growing number of children have no hope of going to school. In some countries, pupils over 12 years of age are not allowed to sit the competitive examination for admission to the first year of the secondary education. Thus, out of 100 children enrolled in 1960, 50 had left school before the end of the primary cycle in the People's Republic of the Congo, Benin, Gabon and in the Libyan Arab Jamahiriya. This wastage reached 60 per cent in Algeria, Burundi and Upper Volta, more than 70 per cent in Botswana, the Central African Republic and Madagascar, and exceeded 80 per cent in Rwanda and Chad.[2] Similar percentages

1. Lè Thành Khôi, op. cit., p. 377.
2. *The Unesco Courier*, June 1972.

are to be found in the dominated countries of South America and Asia. In Africa as a whole, in 1967-68, less than 40 per cent of the children of school age were attending school. In Mauritania, for example, only 10 per cent of the children aged 6 to 12 were in school, only 20 per cent in Mali, Chad, etc. All these children, barely educated or deprived of further schooling, can no longer readapt to their environment. The 'return to the land' and the various kinds of work offered to them or imposed on them cannot satisfy them, because they are too much alive to the difficulties experienced by their parents who are growing cotton, coffee and sisal for starvation wages. So they swell the numbers of the unemployed, underemployed or delinquents; and often they are told that they themselves are responsible for their unemployment.

As for the few young people who, in spite of all, succeed in pursuing their studies, they derive no preparation for life from so doing. This result is essentially attributable to an education which is characterized by:

An excessive dependence in regard to a foreign system (usually that of the former metropolitan State).

The underqualification of primary teachers: teachers are insufficiently paid and do not carry out their work conscientiously; in Africa, the best of them leave teaching to take up responsible administrative posts or political appointments.

The foreign origin of numerous secondary teachers and administrators, as well as of the financial resources.

Curricula drawn up in fact by the ministries concerned with co-operation (in Paris, London, etc.)

The overlong duration of studies.

The use of a foreign language of instruction, and the foreign nature of the content of the subjects taught to pupils. School wastage results also in a need for foreign higher staff and technicians. In some French-speaking countries more than 80 per cent of the posts at managerial and technical level are occupied by foreigners. Even ordinary skilled manpower has to be recruited abroad. Meanwhile, thousands of young people leave school each year without having learnt a trade or possessing the least qualification. What is then advocated is recourse to birth control. For one of the 'causes' of underdevelopment and unemployment to which the ideologists of the 'Third World economy' make most frequent reference is population growth. But nothing could be more ridiculous than this argument in the context of the Third World, and especially in that of Africa, where, apart from a few giants like Nigeria, Egypt and Ethiopia, more than half the countries have a population of only 400,000 to less than 3 million, whereas their area is often greater, and much greater, than a million square kilometres.

Instead of seeking to limit the number of births, what is needed is to make the peoples aware of their plight. They will then succeed in providing work for all social groups (the aged, adults, youth) and later control their own reproduction according to their own needs. Africa needs a larger population, it is vast enough to maintain millions and millions of young people, since it has lost so many in the course of history. There are never too many mouths to feed, for there are always, barring accidents, two arms working for each mouth being fed.

Conclusion

In conclusion, we must once more emphasize the limited character of this study, which aims rather at providing food for reflection on the question of unemployment among educated young people and at setting out some problems which derive from it in the French-speaking developing countries, than at presenting exact quantitative conclusions or complete and structured answers. Our purpose has been to put forward a certain number of working hypotheses calculated to interest both the countries which are particularly hard hit by unemployment among young people holding diplomas or certificates and the organizations which help those countries. To give exact conclusions with precise suggestions, a thorough study would be needed, based on methodical surveys conducted in each of the countries concerned. Every country has its individuality, and the problems arising from unemployment among young people are not necessarily the same in one country as they are in its neighbours.

Nevertheless, it will be noted that unemployment among young people has for some years past been an international reality: it is now rife in all the market-economy countries, whether developed or developing. Consequently, some factors are much the same everywhere, and this applies particularly to the French-speaking countries of the Third World. We shall therefore revert to a few ideas expressed in this study.

In speaking of young people, however, we must know what young people we have in mind. The social origin of young people is determinant in regard to choice of studies, level of education reached and, lastly, choice of occupation. This remains true even though all young people have in common the fact of being the last to arrive on a labour market that is limited, saturated or almost non-existent in certain developing countries. The majority of the pupils' parents are illiterate and their children have to learn to decide for themselves the direction they will follow in choosing an occupation. Most often it is a case of simply imitating or of yielding to the attraction of a picture found in some book. This choice rarely corresponds to employment offers or to the capacity of the labour market. Thus, even those who have been trained, for example, in tool repairing and the use of modern machines (tractors, lorries, etc.) are not all able to find a job suited to their training, because there are still very few machines of this kind in many of the Third World countries. Learning the traditional techniques and forms of labour organization in each country would seem to be more useful as a way of helping to limit unemployment among young people.

In any case, education, as practised in the French-speaking Third World, is not adapted to the new socio-economic situations. It cannot therefore shield from unemployment young people holding diplomas or certificates, whatever their level. Education, which formerly 'manufactured' junior employees for the colonists, or which represented for a few privileged individuals a means of social advancement or 'assimilation', no longer performs this function. It is henceforth considered by some independent countries as an indicator of economic development. This conception of education is bound to have some effects on its content, which moreover corresponds neither to the way of life, nor above all to the labour market, which is very limited in the French-speaking countries. It appears that this content, although not fundamentally the cause of unemployment, plays a particularly important part in the French-speaking countries with a market economy. Foreign companies established in these countries usually either prefer to employ young workers without diplomas or those with a lower diploma because they can pay them less, or else, when they are very modern, find themselves unable to employ holders of higher diplomas who are available on the local market because those diplomas are rarely geared to the sophisticated techniques used by such companies.

Many French-speaking developing countries are caught up in this contradiction, particularly those which are relatively advanced, such as Ivory Coast and Gabon. Consequently, unemployment and underemployment among educated young people worsens from year to year, side by side with the chronic scarcity of specialized workers, skilled workers, higher administrative staff, technicians, managers, etc.

While, in the developed countries with a market economy, it is possible to speak of an 'overproduction' of people holding diplomas, in the developing countries one should rather speak of the maladjustment of education because the diplomas awarded are slanted towards foreign situations and not towards the national economy. African holders of diplomas (doctors, engineers, secondary-school teachers, specialized workers) are better acquainted with the modern techniques determined by the economic level of the developed countries with a market economy than with those that are suited to the economic level of their own country. It is often 'easier' for them to work in a foreign country where there is a labour market consonant with their knowledge, even if they are underemployed or underpaid there, than to work in their own country where they have to start again from the beginning. The imported technologies should be recast in the light of the economic level of each country, and this would require a change in the socio-political conditions and a review of the relations with developed countries and multinational corporations. In this regard, the problems posed by 'the transfer of technology' or 'the transfer of knowledge' must not be overlooked. Unemployment among holders of diplomas—and even unemployment in general—is closely connected with the labour market as well as with the market of the technology that these countries must acquire.

A few words should also perhaps be said about the inability of the economic system of the countries with which we are concerned in this study to provide work for young people—an inability due to the relations of dependence which they have with the developed countries and especially with the multinational corporations.

While unemployment among adults and young people has, in the developed countries and in the Third World, the same function from the point of view of capital (that is to say, to assist capitalist growth and accumulation), this function is apparent in a specific way in the Third World countries because of their dependence. Unemployment helps to maintain low wages, reduce production costs, promote a constant redistribution of the labour force throughout the world and a concentration of capitalist enterprises in places where 'social peace' seems to reign, with the result that young educated people who are unemployed have to emigrate so as to work where there are factories.

In order to gain an understanding of the phenomenon of unemployment in these countries, it is necessary to start from the relations they have with the developed countries, and especially with the multinational corporations whose economic policies are so often contrary to their interests. These relations determine the whole political and economic context, and it is from them that stems, in the last analysis, unemployment among young people. Thus, education, most often planned abroad and imposed through the system of aid and co-operation between different countries, can only produce young educated people who will not find work, and who will become ever more numerous in the future. Permanent unemployment among young people, and especially among educated young people, which has been increasing for some years past, is caused, on the one hand, by the organization, content and cost of education, and, on the other, by the policy of foreign enterprises which most often are glad to have a large reserve of unqualified manpower (the cost price of which is lower and enables them to make huge profits) or which prefer to import from abroad their higher staff, their technicians and their skilled workers (whose training has cost them nothing). This gives rise to a situation where the foreign and the indigenous populations are in competition and where the latter are always the losers. It can then be said that unemployment in Africa—and in the Third World in general—is essentially political since, at the worst, it is deliberately brought about by the great multinational corporations with the aim of producing cheaply in those countries and selling more expensively elsewhere.

It may also be said that, on account of their socio-economic condition, some developing countries arouse feelings of greed in certain developed countries rather than a will to help. J. C. Pomonti is thus justified in writing:

The African continent offers a rather impressive number of records: underpopulation, natural wealth, youth, political refugees, aridity, social under-development, economic dependence. These particulars explain the cupidity of which it is the subject, and the wars, open or masked, of which it is the scene, at a time when decolonization is uncompleted.[1]

This cupidity has effects on the labour market and on the money market, inside and outside the developing countries. As the latter turn over to the rich countries, by way of repayment of their debts, more money than they receive from those countries, their economy is in a state of total dependence. The former director of the World Bank, Mr Woods, thus noted that 'the financing of development is, for many countries, a disguised subsidy for their exports'.[2] The funds allotted to a State must be used to pay for its purchases in the donor country. Accordingly, the aid granted in the context of international co-operation enriches the wealthiest countries and impoverishes the poorest countries. It should be added that the latter also incur prestige expenditure which in no way creates new jobs. Even the aid accorded in respect of the training of higher staff or of instructors is bound to raise problems, for it is not adapted to the needs and socio-economic situations of the countries which receive this aid. What is needed is not to transmit a Western model, since this leads to the multiplication of people with diplomas for whom no jobs can be found, but to infuse vitality into the traditional structures of employment. Moreover, plans for development or for the training of higher staff, generally drawn up by foreign experts and outside the countries concerned, do not take account of the traditional techniques of each country, whereas promoting these techniques would be the best way to ensure the assimilation of foreign modern technology. This technology, imported just as it

1. J. C. Pomonti, 'Une Décolonisation Tardive et Inachevée, *Le Monde* (Paris), 10-11 October 1976, p. 19.

2. Quoted by René Monory in 'Pour une Nouvelle Attitude de la Coopération', *Le Monde* (Paris), 7 August 1976, p. 4.

is, always has the effect in the developing countries of creating a void in the labour market, a lack of qualified manpower which also has to be imported from abroad, while thousands of young people are unemployed or underemployed in the home country.

The result is as follows: 300 million people were jobless or underemployed in the Third World in 1975, according to the International Labour Office which rightly calls in question in this connection the whole content of education. 'There is a kind of cannibalism in this', writes Louis Emmerj, head of the Employment and Development Department of ILO. 'Each level of study is designed to prepare for the following level, but not to be put to use. A whole pyramid pushes towards the top two or three pupils who are more gifted or more fortunate.' [1]

To reduce the number of unemployed among young people holding diplomas or certificates in French-speaking developing countries, some experts [2] advocate curbing the extension of education in order to improve its content, the standard of the pupils, and adaptation to local situations. In reality, improvement of the content of education cannot follow from a reduction in the number of pupils, which is relatively low in many French-speaking countries. Reducing the number of pupils of course means diminishing the number of unemployed holders of diplomas or certificates, but it also means increasing the number of uneducated unemployed. Nor can demography be evoked in this regard. In these countries, the population is neither numerous nor dense. Consequently, the policy of birth control, as applied in certain developing countries, cannot really solve the problem of unemployment among young people from within nor can it improve the content of education; it chiefly affects poor families and in no way provides work for the young 'survivors'. The French-speaking Third World, which is under-populated, cannot afford this solution. Furthermore, it is usually the economic level and the exploitation of the masses that lead to uncontrolled procreation.

In the last analysis, the problem of unemployment among young people holding diplomas or certificates, in French-speaking

1. Quoted by Joanine Roy in *Le Monde* (Paris), 18 March 1975, p. 18.
2. See Round Table held at Dakar on education from 7-12 February 1972.

Africa and elsewhere, like many other problems which these countries have to face, is above all a problem inherent in the way chosen for economic development. It is therefore important that each country, each government, when it is led to demand the stabilization of prices of raw materials, monetary reform, the reform of news information procedures, the right to advanced technology, etc., should not confine itself to the purely technical aspects of prices, currency, information, etc., but should endeavour to bring about a complete change in its structures, taking account of the aspirations, the right to work, and the minimum living wage of workers. To this end, even in present conditions, it would be desirable, as regards unemployment among holders of diplomas and certificates, to study in each country the part played by the wage structure in the utilization of qualified workers (national or foreign) and in their distribution within the national economy, to examine the wage differentials of holders of diplomas and certificates according to the different levels and types of education, and their relation with the different economic sectors likely to ensure the national economic development. It appears that several developing countries, besides their dependence on the rich countries—or because of this dependence—know little about the operation of their own labour market, more particularly the procedures of supply and demand concerning workers holding diplomas or certificates and the utilization in one form or another of qualified manpower. The methods which they apply to predict their needs for qualified manpower and to determine the objectives of education in the light of the objectives of the national economic development, are also very inadequate. They usually do no more than copy imported methods which are not in keeping with the level and structure of their national economy.

In any case, the problem of unemployment among young people throws fresh light on the economic difficulties of the Third World countries, and reveals the consequences of their dependence in regard to the developed countries with a market economy. On the proper solution of this problem will depend the future of these Third World countries, for they have many young people, and youth represents the future.

Bibliography

INDIVIDUAL OR JOINT WORKS

Arnin, S. *Impérialisme et Sous-développement en Afrique.* Anthropos, Paris, 1976. 440 p.

—— · *Accumulation à l'Échelle Mondiale.* Anthropos, Paris, 1970. 589 p.

Austruy, J. *Le Scandale du Développement, Bilans de la Connaissance Économique.* Paris, Marcel Rivière, 1965. 527 p.

Bairoch, P. *Urban Unemployment in the Developing Countries.* Geneva, International Labour Office, 1972. 106 p.

Bartoli, H; Salomon, Ph. *Théorie Économique et Stratégie d'Enseignement.* Paris, Librairie Générale de Droit et de Jurisprudence, 1967. 219 p.

Freyssenet, M. *Le Processus de Déqualification, Surqualification de la Force de Travail.* Paris, Centre de Sociologie Urbaine, 1974, 248 p.

Hugon, P. *Analyse du Sous-Développpment en Afrique Noire: Exemple de l'Economie du Cameroun.* Paris, Presses Universitaires de France, 1968. 327 p.

International Labour Office. *Employment in Africa: Critical Aspects of the Problem.* Geneva, 1973. 309 p.

—— · *Quatrième Conférence Régionale Africaine (Nairobi, nov.-déc. 1973). Rapport II: Emploi, Statut et Conditions des Travailleurs Migrants et des autres Travailleurs Possédant la Nationalité d'autres Pays Africains,* Geneva, 1973. 98 p.

—— · *Troisième Conférence Régionale Africaine (Accra, décembre 1969). Rapport IV: La Politique et l'Emploi en Afrique, partie I, Problèmes et Politiques.* Geneva, 1969. 137 p.

International Labour Office; Unesco Regional Office for Education in Africa. *Population, Education and Development in Africa South of the Sahara 1971.* Geneva, 1971. 173 p.

Mazouni, A. *Culture et Enseignement en Algérie et Maghreb.* Paris, Maspero, 1969. 247 p.

Michon, F. *Chômeurs et Chômage.* Paris, Presses Universitaires de France, 1975. 290 p. (Publications de l'Université de Paris I Panthèon-Sorbonne). (Sciences Économiques.)

Ministry of the Civil Service and Labour. Benin. *La Situation de l'Emploi dans le Secteur Moderne de l'Économie du Bénin. Prévisions 1975-1978*. No. 2 Cotonou, April 1975. 306 p.

Moumouni, A. *L'Education en Afrique*. Paris, Maspero, 1964. 425 p.

Quandet, L. *La Responsabilité de la Langue Française dans l'Échec Scolaire en République Centrafricaine*. Paris, 1972. 91 p. (Mémoire de maîtrise de l'Université de Paris X.)

Unesco Regional Office for Education in Africa. *Une autre Education pour la Jeunesse? Formation—Action pour le Développement*. Dakar, 1972. 267 p.

Zoctizoum, Y. *Idéologies et Transformations due Milieu Rural en République Centrafricaine*. Paris, 1972. 202 p. (Mémoire de maîtrise de l'Université de Paris X.)

PERIODICALS

Costa, E. Employment Problems and Policies in Senegal. *International Labour Review*, Vol. 95, No. 5, May 1967, p. 417-51.

——. Practical Aspects of the Organization of Manpower Utilization and Education Schemes in the Developing Countries. *International Labour Review*, Vol. 93, No. 3, March 1966, p. 248-80.

Hugon, P. La Planification de l'Enseignement et de l'Emploi en Afrique Noire et à Madagascar. *Revue Économique de Madagascar*, 6 January 1971, p. 265-315.

Hunter, G. Employment Policy in Tropical Africa: The Need for Radical Revision. *International Labour Review*, Vol. 105, No. 1, January 1972, p. 39-65.

Kailas, C; Galles, H. Size and Characteristics of Wage Employment in Africa: Some Statistical Estimates. *International Labour Review*, Vol. 93, No. 2, February 1966, p. 149-73.

Lè Thành Khôi, L'Enseignement en Afrique Noire. *Revue Tiers-Monde 1971*. Paris, Presses Universitaires de France, 1971. 463 p.

Lobstein, P. Prerequisites for a Rural Employment Policy in French-speaking Black Africa. *International Labour Review*, Vol. 102, No. 2 August 1970. p. 141-89.

Roussel, L. Measuring Rural-Urban Drift in Developing Countries: A Suggested Method. *International Labour Review*, Vol. 101, No. 2, March 1970, p. 229-46.

Rousset, P. Emigration. Paupérisation et Développement du Capitalisme d'État en Algérie. *Revue Contradictions* (Brussels), special number 1975, 112 p.

Seers, D. New Light on Structural Unemployment: Lessons of a Mission to Ceylon. *International Labour Review*, Vol. 105, No. 2, February 1972, p. 99-108.

Thormann, P. The Rural-Urban Income Differential and Minimum Wage Fixing Criteria. *International Labour Review*, Vol. 102, No. 2, August 1970, p. 127-47.

Vigno, J. Le Commerce Entre Pays Africains. *Le Monde* (Paris), 10-11 October 1976, p. 17.

[A.15] SS.78/D.103/A.